College and University

BUDGETING

An Introduction for Faculty And Academic Administrators

Second Edition

Richard J. Meisinger, Jr.

NACUBO

Library of Congress Cataloging-in-Publication Data

Meisinger, Richard J., 1945–
    College and university budgeting: an introduction for faculty and
academic administrators / Richard J. Meisinger, Jr. — 2nd ed.
        p.   cm.
    Includes bibliographical references and index.
    ISBN: 0-915164-94-9: $60.00
    1. Universities and colleges—United States—Finance.
    2. Universities and colleges—United States—Business management.
    I. Title
    LB2342.M43   1994
    378'.02'0973—dc20   94-20513
                                                                CIP

© Copyright 1994 by the National Association of
College and University Business Officers
One Dupont Circle
Washington, DC 20036

Edited by Deirdre M. Greene
Designed by Stacey Trey

Contents

Preface

Once upon a time in a large city zoo a lion cub was placed in a cage next to a grizzled old-timer of a lion. The zookeeper came by at feeding time the first evening with her food wagon and tossed the old lion a huge piece of sirloin steak and the cub a pile of hay. The cub looked at the pile of hay for a moment, eyed what remained of the steak on the floor of the old lion's cage, and called after the zookeeper, "There's been some mistake here!" But the zookeeper ignored the cub and continued on her rounds.

The pattern was repeated the second and third evenings: sirloin steak for the lion, and a pile of hay for the cub. By this time the lion cub was beside himself with rage. He bellowed, "I can't live on hay! I need red meat!" The zookeeper continued to ignore him, but the old lion asked, "Hey kid, what's bothering you?" The young lion said, "There's been some terrible mistake. I'm a young, virile cub and I need red meat so I can grow. But I only get hay. Instead, they give the steak to you, an old-timer in his declining years." The old lion smiled and shook his head sagely. "Kid, there's been no mistake here. It's just that you're being carried on the budget as a zebra."

The budgets of higher education institutions can be every bit as baffling to the uninitiated as the zoo's budget was to the lion cub. This puzzlement has been magnified by the tremendous turbulence in the national economy in the early 1990s. In addition, several factors have combined to increase the financial pressures on higher education: higher education's priority on the national social agenda has been sliding for the last two decades; and productivity gains have been elusive in the people-intensive enterprise of higher education, with the consequence that resources available to most institutions have become scarcer than in years past.

The primary audiences for this primer are new academic administrators and faculty members who seek a more active role in campus governance and therefore need a greater knowledge of administrative processes, particularly about budgets and budgeting. The book should also be useful to seasoned campus financial and academic officers who wish to be sensitized to the role of faculty in the budget process.

After perusing this book, readers should gain sufficient understanding of the budget process to be able to phrase academic questions in terms of budgets and the process and to become more constructive and knowledgeable participants in the budgetary process. This increased sophistication should lead to improved communication among participants in the budgetary process and should reduce the tension that often accompanies budgeting. The book also should enable faculty to identify better the issues with significant budgetary consequences and therefore to influence the budgetary process and its outcomes.

Chapter 1 is an introduction to budgets and the budgetary process, with a brief explanation of why budgeting is an important element of policy making. The chapter answers a number of questions frequently asked by those unfamiliar with budgeting: What is a budget? Is a budget more than an incomprehensible document filled with columns of numbers? Why do budgeting? What, in a technical sense, makes up a budget?

Chapter 2 discusses the broader economic and political contexts of budgeting and describes the framework for the budgetary process both on and off campus. The importance of enrollments as a major factor in resource issues is highlighted. The various sources of funds for both public and independent institutions are identified. Questions about the effects of political and economic factors on institutional budgets are answered: For what goods and services do institutions expend their resources? Do the costs of these goods and services increase faster for higher education than for other sectors of the economy? What specific social and political factors, such a demographics, concern for student access, and federal legislation, directly influence institutional budgets? How do state and local governments differ with respect to wealth, willingness to tax wealth, and the proportion of taxes directed toward higher education? To what extent do public and independent institutions differ in their sources of revenues?

Chapter 3 identifies factors that distinguish the budgetary process of one institution from that of another. The concept of roles is discussed to provide a simple framework for understanding budget behavior at various levels of the budgetary process. The capital budget and the relationship between the operating budget and the capital budget are explained. To illustrate the complexity and overlap of budget cycles, multiyear summaries of the budgetary process in different types of institutions are presented. Finally, the principal participants in budgeting are identified and the chronology of the operating and the capital budgetary processes are discussed for both public and independent institutions.

Chapter 3 seeks to answer the following questions: How does an institution's character shape the budgetary process? How can faculty and administrators participate more actively in the budgetary process? How do the roles of participants in the budgetary process affect their expectations? Why are operating budgets largely determined two years ahead, and capital budgets up to five years ahead? To what extent is participation in the budgetary process constrained by the schedule of budget development? At what stages of the budgetary process are participation by faculty more likely? What do decision makers consider when they prepare and review budgets?

Chapter 4 describes how participants influence the operating and capital budgetary processes. The principal focus of the chapter is flexibility, which, accompanied by the ability to maneuver within a system of constraints, is necessary for effective management. Many budgeters consider flexibility the central concept in budgeting. The relationship between risk and budgets is discussed, and several key decision points are described. By focusing time and energy on these decision points, policy makers can magnify their influence in the budgetary process. Constraints experienced by budgeters are identified, and strategies are suggested for increasing flexibility. How changes in institutional character can influence the budgetary process is discussed. Some of the major policy issues confronting public institutions and state officials are identified. Chapter 4 attempts to answer questions frequently raised by faculty and administrators at department and college levels: How are faculty salary adjustment pools determined each year? How is faculty workload commonly measured? How are budget allocations made among departments or colleges? How can resources be obtained for a particular department or college? Why is it important to conform to seemingly cumbersome institutional accounting procedures? What effect does collective bargaining have on the budgetary process?

Chapter 5 discusses the sensitive issue of budgetary planning for reallocation and retrenchment. This subject is all the more pressing because of the financial reversals experienced by many institutions during the early 1990s. The least disruptive reallocation and retrenchment strategies tend to be those implemented in anticipation of fiscal stringency or to

meet a need to reorder institutional priorities. The range of options and
the flexibility available to an institution are limited in the midst of a financial crisis. The experiences of participants in several institutions that
have suffered fiscal reversals or major changes in priorities are cited to
identify the major considerations in these situations. Also, several short-
term, intermediate-term, and long-term strategies for coping with retrenchment and reallocation are examined. These strategies are
applicable to both public and independent institutions.

This volume is not intended to be a comprehensive discussion of financing and budgeting in colleges and universities. Participants in the
budgetary process who do not have primary responsibility for budgeting
generally have limited time to devote to the process. It seems reasonable
to expect them to focus on the policy issues arising from the budgetary
process rather than to immerse themselves in technical detail. As participants become more familiar and more comfortable with the process,
however, they probably will begin to delve more into the technical
aspects.

It is not possible here to do justice to the unique character of each of
the nations's more than 3,000 institutions of higher education and on
the budgetary process at each institution. Many institutions have strong
traditions that account for enormous differences in the ways faculty, administrators, and students participate in the budgetary process. In addition, the distinction between public and independent institutions is
becoming blurred. Many public institutions receive a smaller proportion
of their funding from state governments now than they did a decade
ago. Public institutions have become much more aggressive about fund
raising from private sources, while independent institutions are recipients of considerable governmental aid. Accordingly, this introduction to
the process must be interpreted by the reader in the context of his or her
own institution's unique character.

Acknowledgments, Second Edition

NACUBO has aggressively supported this book during the 10 years since the first edition was published. NACUBO President Caspa L. Harris Jr.'s belief that this volume still carries an important message for faculty and administrators is a guiding force behind this revised second edition.

The second edition bears the imprint of dozens of faculty and administrative colleagues across the country who, over the past decade, have offered suggestions for improving the organization, strengthening the arguments, and clarifying the text. Anthony B. Flores of the University of California, Davis brought me up to date on the latest changes in accounting procedures for nonprofit organizations. I am especially grateful to Richard Anderson, Washington University; Ernst Benjamin, American Association of University Professors (AAUP); Stephen D. Campbell, Clinch Valley College; Anna Marie Cirino, NACUBO; Nathan Dickmeyer, City University of New York; Don Hood, Columbia University; and Jack H. Schuster, Claremont Graduate School for reviewing a draft of the second edition and offering constructive criticisms that have considerably improved this book. I, of course, take responsibility for any errors or omissions.

The production of this edition could not have happened without the adept guidance of my editor, Deirdre M. Greene. She served as both taskmaster and friend, gently pushing the book along from outline to finished draft. Her advice was invaluable throughout the process. Lou Bates, my able executive assistant, patiently assembled the many drafts of the book as we moved through increasingly sophisticated versions of word processing software.

Acknowledgments for the First Edition

While preparing this book, we received the support of a number of individuals without whose interest our work would have suffered. We are indebted to these persons.

Stephen D. Campbell, then director of NACUBO's Financial Management Center, developed the original proposal for this book and coordinated the project through its first phases. His successor at NACUBO, James A. Hyatt, ably continued in the role as project coordinator. Irving J. Spitzberg, Jr., then general secretary of AAUP, strongly supported the concept of a joint AAUP-NACUBO approach to the preparation of this book. D. F. Finn, then executive vice president of NACUBO, generously offered encouragement in the belief that better understanding of the budget process and of the faculty's role in it would benefit every institution.

Funds for this project were provided by the Exxon Education Foundation.

A key role in the conceptualizing and preparation of this book was played by an advisory panel composed of AAUP and NACUBO representatives: David J. Berg, University of Minnesota; Claude Campbell, City University of New York; Donald C. Cell, Cornell College; Elmer Jagow, Hiram College; Mary M. Lai, Long Island University; and Jon C. Liebman, University of Illinois, Urbana-Champaign. These individuals generously gave considerable time to reviewing the book in its many stages.

Early drafts of this book were reviewed by a number of our colleagues and many suggestions were received for improvement of the manuscript. In particular, we wish to thank the following persons for stimulating out thinking: Frederick R. Ford, Purdue University; W. C. Freeman, The Texas A & M University System; Lyman A. Glenny, University of California, Berkeley; Marilyn McCoy, University of Colorado; James R. Mingle, Southern Regional Education Board; Louis W. Moelchert Jr., University of Richmond; Anthony W. Morgan, University of Utah; Michael L. Shattock, University of Warwick; Paul Strohm, Indiana University; Aaron Wildavsky, University of California, Berkeley; and Robert O. Berdahl, Stewart L. Edelstein, Allen Schick, Frank A. Schmidtlein, and Charles F. Sturtz, University of Maryland, College Park. Also, Ralph S. Brown, Jr., Yale University, discussed with us the

AAUP definitions of financial exigency, and Ilona Turrisi, Florida State University, provided some case materials for departmental budgeting.

We are also indebted to Marjorie Huseman and Virgina Obermeier for typing and proofreading many drafts of this book.

ONE
Introduction

The budget has many roles (see figure 1.1) that significantly impact daily institutional life. A corporate executive once noted, "Nothing gets done if it's not in the budget!"

Clearly, budgets would be unnecessary if sufficient resources were available to satisfy the needs of everyone in an institution. Only an accounting system would be needed to track allocations and expenditures. However, resources will always be insufficient to meet existing demands; therefore, a budget becomes a mechanism for setting priorities. Incorporating the consideration of alternative expenditure plans, the budget summarizes which and at what financial levels activities will be supported. If additional resources become available, it may be possible to engage in more activities or to support the activities high on the priority list in grander fashion; if fewer resources become available, it may be necessary to engage in fewer activities or to reduce support for activities low on the priority list.

Figure 1.1   The Roles of the Budget

- ☐ A mechanism for setting priorities
- ☐ An institutional plan of action
- ☐ An institutional contract
- ☐ A control mechanism
- ☐ A gauge of risk
- ☐ An instrument of communication
- ☐ A political device

Similarly, a budget is a plan of action for the institution. The budget represents a list of proposed activities with price tags. As the budget cycle progresses, the nature of the activities and the estimates of expenditures may change, but the budget continues to provide the overall sense of direction for the institution. The budget also provides coherence to interdependent activities, from academic departments to administrative support services and research programs.

If the budget is a plan of action, it is also a form of contract. In the public arena, a state government appropriates funds for colleges and universities with the expectation that the institutions will provide certain instructional, research, and public services. With enrollments as the principal determinant of funding levels in public institutions, the state provides its allocations with the understanding that institutions will educate agreed-upon numbers of students. In both public and independent institutions, academic departments are allocated a share of the available resources with the understanding that faculty will teach a specified schedule of courses, counsel students, perform department-sponsored research, and engage in public service. Academic and support departments expect to be funded at certain levels in return for the services they provide. The budget is a summary of commitments made by both the funding agency and the recipient of those funds. From this implicit contractual understanding arises the expectation of accountability.

The budget can be viewed as a control mechanism. The flow of resources to activities is regulated in accordance with institutional objectives. Once resources have been allocated, their expenditure can be monitored and checked for conformity with plans and expectations. To ensure accountability, operating units whose expenditures deviate from the plan should be asked to justify the differences. Significant but appropriate deviations might be signals to modify the budget plan during the next budget cycle.

The budget is a gauge of the amount of risk that institutional decision makers are willing to tolerate. Because the budget is a plan, it is founded on a number of assumptions about income streams and expenditure patterns. Conservative budgeters incorporate assumptions that allow for greater disturbances to resource flows than do aggressive budgeters.

As a network of communication, the budget is often the best way for an operating unit, department, or institution to express its objectives and to identify the resources needed to meet those objectives. Most budget requests are reviewed at roughly the same time so that judgments can be made about competing activities. Decisions about how many resources a unit or institution is to receive are also a form of communication as to how the activities of that unit or institution are valued by decision makers at higher levels. The budget also informs people about the activities of units at a "distance" from their own units. Department chairs, for example, might not ordinarily have much day-to-day contact with the physical plant operations staff, but can appreciate the scope and complexity of those operations by reviewing their budgets.

Changes in the budget from one cycle to another also communicate information about changes in priorities among activities and about changes in the availability of resources. These changes are especially important in that the budget is, among other things, an accumulation of historical obligations. Within a budget cycle the monitoring of expenditure patterns provides information about how the institution and its operating units are adapting to unanticipated changes in the environment.

Above all, the budget is a political device. It reflects the outcome of a series of negotiations over which activities should be funded and at what levels. To create the budget, administrators from various departments strike bargains and make trade-offs. Participants in the budgetary process assert their leadership and influence to bring about changes in the distribution of resources. Because two or three budget cycles are always under consideration at any time, the results of negotiations over the budget for one cycle have an effect on the negotiations over the budgets of other cycles. As in any negotiation, the demands of one side are never completely satisfied. However, through the negotiation process participants can effectively communicate their demands for services and their resource needs. Out of this process, too, should come a better understanding of other activities competing for the same scarce resources. Negotiations over resources can be acrimonious, but, if structured properly, they should lead to consensus building both within the institution and between the institution and its funding sources.

Budgeting as an Ongoing Process

No sooner does a budget document roll off the printing presses than the commitments in it change. Because the budget is an attempt to plan expenditures and forecast income, and because such plans and forecasts cannot anticipate all future events, the budget generally undergoes revision as it is implemented. Thus, budgeting is a process that does not end with the assembly of a budget document.

The single most important determinant of the budget for a given cycle is the budget for the previous cycle. Budgets represent a consolidation of decisions made earlier about the institution or its operating units; budgets tend to be altered incrementally to reflect marginal changes from one cycle to another. The budget for a particular budget cycle portrays an institution of a certain size; with a certain distribution of faculty salaries, ages, and tenure statuses; with a certain student body of a given geographical distribution and academic and extracurricular interests; with a certain location; with a certain mission; and with a certain institutional "character." Because the nature of the institution changes, albeit slowly, the composition of its budget must change too.

Budgets are designed to anticipate as well as possible any fluctuations in the institution's fiscal fortune so that faculty and administrators are not surprised by surpluses or deficits. At the same time, the budget must be flexible enough to allow institutional officials to respond to changes in the environment. Flexibility usually comes from "slack" resources, that is, available resources that have not been committed for other purposes. The management of these flexible resources during the budget cycle is an important element of the budget process.

In summary, a budget is never "still." Budgeting should be viewed as a dynamic consensus-building process that involves all key institutional decision makers.

Why Do Budgeting?

Budgeting as we know it is a relatively recent practice begun in the late 19th century. For centuries before, a "budget" was nothing more than a leather pouch in which the king or government official kept the receipts of taxation or the spoils of war or other sources of revenue, and from which he withdrew funds for his expenditure. The budget evolved into an expenditure plan as life grew more complex and it became necessary to anticipate the future costs of operations and to compare those costs with expected revenues. The budget became a method for dealing with present and future problems in an organized fashion and for reducing uncertainty. As the statement of needs often exceeded available resources, the budget also became a forum for setting priorities.

Institutions of higher education have extremely complex fiscal underpinnings. Stanford University, for example, has approximately 8,000 income accounts, most of them restricted to specific purposes (e.g., research grant and contract funds can be applied only toward the project for which they are awarded; gifts earmarked for a particular function can be used only for that purpose; and revenue from the purchase of time on an institution's nuclear reactor must be used to operate and maintain the facility). The budgetary process is now the means for planning and tracking revenues and expenditures so that resources can be used most effectively to meet the institution's educational goals as well as to comply with contracts that limit the use of the income.

The management of resources serves at least two important functions. First, it satisfies the accountability requirement that unrestricted funds be spent properly according to the institution's legal framework and goals. In this capacity, the budget serves as a control mechanism. An underlying issue is the delicate balance between accountability to the source of income and institutional autonomy and academic freedom. Second, the managers of resources recognize that several activities directly depend on certain restricted or designated funds. Administrators and faculty must realize that as funds decrease or disappear, the activities supported by these funds must be curtailed or eliminated.

Components of the Budget

Budgeting as a process of negotiation is also a means of deciding "fair shares," an ambiguous but important concept indicating how operating units or institutions stand relative to one another in the distribution of resources. The term fair share does not necessarily imply a proportional distribution of increases or decreases in resources. No participants in the budgetary process ever receive as many resources as they could possibly use, but they are generally satisfied with their allocation if they perceive that relative to other participants they are treated equitably. If the reasons for the unequal distribution of resources are known and generally accepted, participants will tend to perceive that they have received fair shares of the resource pool. The extent to which participants believe that they have received fair shares is also a measure of the perceived legitimacy of the process through which resources are allocated and, more broadly, of the entire decision-making process.

The preparation of a budget should be viewed as an opportunity for individuals and agencies with a commitment to the institution to examine institutional programs and activities. Although the operations of the institution are continuous, they can be rechanneled through changes in the budget. Because of the direct relationship between program operations and resources, the review of program priorities must be translated at some point into the language of dollars. Thus, fiscal decisions have academic implications, just as academic decisions have fiscal implications.

What Makes Up a Budget?

In any institution of higher education, there are generally several different kinds of budgets concurrently in operation. Faculty and administrators at the departmental level may be affected directly by only some of these budgets that together make up the institution's total budget. Following are the different components:

☐ Operating budgets
☐ Capital budgets
☐ Restricted budgets
☐ Auxiliary enterprise budgets
☐ Hospital operations budgets
☐ Service center budgets

These budget types may be characterized differently at many institutions. The broadest and most frequently encountered designations are the operating budget and the capital budget. The other components may be subsets of these but are discussed separately here because of their unique characteristics.

The operating budget generally includes all of the regular unrestricted income available to the institution plus those restricted funds (e.g., endowed professorships and sponsored programs) that are earmarked for instructional activities and departmental support. Activities included in the operating budget are the basic expenses of departments, schools, and colleges, including personnel and day-to-day operating costs; student services; libraries; administration; campus operations and maintenance (i.e., facilities operation); development; and the unrestricted portion of endowment income, gifts, and student aid. Although the operating budget is interconnected with other budgets and is therefore not independent, it is usually viewed as the core budget. Because the operating budget includes all unrestricted income, it is the budget most responsive to decisions about changes in program priorities.

The capital budget generally covers expenditures for the construction or renovation of major facilities. The enormous cost of many projects that entail new construction or significant renovations often dictates that these projects be funded through debt financing. In the public sector, this debt is usually managed through a capital budget that is distinct from the operating budget. Recent changes in accounting standards for independent institutions will force the merger of capital and operating budgets as debt service is treated as an operating expense.

There is an obvious but often overlooked relationship between the capital budget and the operating budget: as new facilities are placed in operation, funds are required to equip, heat, light, and maintain them. Renovated facilities that take advantage of recent technological advances may be less expensive to heat and maintain than they were prior to renovation. These factors should be anticipated when developing the capital budget and should be incorporated in the appropriate operating budget.

Restricted budgets usually encompass federally sponsored research grants and contracts, nongovernmental grants, certain endowment and gift income, and student aid from external sources. One example of how the operating budget is linked with the restricted budgets is the relationship of instructional programs to sponsored research programs, which provide support for graduate students involved in research. Funding for the direct costs of research contracts and grants is restricted revenue, whereas reimbursement for indirect costs (i.e., overhead) is unrestricted revenue. An important aspect of much restricted income is its limited duration. Thus, the restricted portion of an institution's total budget is often subject to greater uncertainty than are other portions of the budget.

Auxiliary enterprises are those activities that support the institution but are financially self-contained and specific enough to be managed as separate budget items. Each auxiliary enterprise has a source of income derived from students and, in some cases, the general public. Examples of such activities are residence and dining halls, student union retail activities, intercollegiate athletics, bookstores, and college or university presses.

Normally, auxiliary enterprise funds can be transferred to education and general funds. However, there are several caveats. Some states prohibit these transfers in public institutions. The transfers may lead to unexpected tax implications. Furthermore, all costs, including depreciation, must be moved to auxiliary enterprise accounts before any surpluses are transferred out.

Another type of auxiliary enterprise is a teaching hospital affiliated with an institution. The hospital operating budget encompasses the noninstructional components of the operations of the teaching hospital, to the extent that the instructional and noninstructional costs of medical or health services training can be separately identified.

Service centers are units in the institution that are established primarily to provide services within the institution that receive most or all of their income from internal sources. These units include central word processing facilities, campus stores, photography and reproduction, and physical plant shops. Units treated as service centers have their own internal budgets but are not included in the institution's total budget because they charge other offices and departments within the institution for their services. From an accounting perspective these transactions are, for the most part, internal transfers of funds.

For Further Reading

The best single introduction to budgeting is Aaron Wildavsky's *The New Politics of the Budgetary Process*, 2nd ed. (New York: HarperCollins, 1992), which went through numerous editions before "new" was added to the title. Although this book concentrates on budgeting at the federal level, the principles apply to budgeting in all settings. This book is essential reading for those who wish to become active participants in the budgetary process.

An excellent overview of budgeting in higher education is the chapter by William F. Lasher and Deborah L. Greene, "College and University Budgeting: What Do We Know? What Do We Need to Know?" in John C. Smart, ed., *Higher Education: Handbook of Theory and Research*,

Vol. IX (Edison, NJ: Agathon Press, 1993). Lasher and Greene also provide an extensive list of references.

Anthony W. Morgan examines the assumptions about resource decision making in "The New Strategies: Roots, Context, and Overview," in Larry L. Leslie, ed., *Responding to New Realities in Funding*, New Directions for Institutional Research no. 43 (San Francisco: Jossey-Bass Inc., 1984). Morgan brings political science and organizational theories to bear on the question of how resources are allocated. This is not an introductory article; the reader should have some knowledge of decision-making theory and budgeting.

Although published 15 years ago, J. Kent Caruthers and Melvin Orwig, *Budgeting in Higher Education*, AAHE/ERIC Higher Education Research Report no. 3 (Washington, DC: American Association for Higher Education, 1979) still provides a good overview of budgeting as it relates to higher education. A bit dated, but well written and useful is *Colleges and Money: A Faculty Guide to Academic Economics*, prepared by the *Change* Panel on Academic Economics (New York: *Change Magazine and Educational Change*, 1976).

TWO

The Economic
And Political Environment

An institution's budget is subject to general economic and political climates. Most of these external forces are beyond the control of individual institutions or even the national higher education community. Accordingly, institutional budgeters must anticipate changes in economic and political conditions that may influence the income available to the institution and the costs the institution may have to bear. Unless an institution's budget can withstand continuous strains from outside forces, the institution cannot survive.

The economic changes experienced by higher education beginning in the early 1980s, for example, had a marked impact on all institutions. In many respects these changes reflect a sea change in the nation's support for higher education. Higher education no longer enjoys the very high ranking on national, state, and local societal agendas that it gained in the 1960s. With competing demands such as corrections, health, welfare, and environmental oversight edging past higher education on most governmental priority lists, public and independent institutions alike must compete for fewer public resources; in the face of costs that increase, on average, faster than the Consumer Price Index (CPI), institutions must charge students higher tuition and fees. Few colleges or universities have been spared these economic pressures. Many public institutions have had to curtail program offerings, increase faculty workloads, and reduce support staff to cope with the twin dilemmas of increasing costs and decreasing resources. Even relatively wealthy Ivy League institutions such as Yale University and the University of Pennsylvania have had to retrench permanently.

11

National Economic and Political Factors

Macroeconomic Environment

The economies of all higher education institutions are intertwined with the economy of the United States, which is increasingly connected to a world economy. Some of these macroeconomic issues set the boundaries for the economies of institutions. The purpose here is not to provide a primer on macroeconomics or to offer economic projections, but rather to highlight some of the relationships between the national economy and institutional policy. Projections are best left to the economists.

National productivity, the federal budget deficit, and the national trade deficit are three important interrelated aspects of the national economy whose impact is felt at the institutional level. Much attention has been given to the size of the national budget deficit. The deficit is large, but not disproportionately so compared with other major economies worldwide. Thus, a number of economists believe that the effects of the deficit on the economy are manageable. The larger the deficit, the more resources must be directed to servicing the debt instead of to capital investments. If the national economy is growing sufficiently, however, enough resources become available both to service the national debt and to invest in new technologies and equipment.

As discussed by Richard Anderson and Joel Meyerson, the gross national product (GNP), the aggregate measure of the total goods and services produced by the economy, grew by about 3 percent per year (above inflation) on average during the 1960s, 1970s, and 1980s, although the rate slowly diminished during the 1970s and 1980s. In the United States, the standard of living for most individuals and families did not keep pace with expectations between 1975 and 1990. Productivity, usually the engine that improves the standard of living, lagged during the same period. To compensate, the United States borrowed heavily, especially in the 1980s: consumer debt increased from 60 percent of GNP in 1980 to 80 percent of GNP in 1988. The flip side of this trend is that the U.S. savings rate is one of the lowest of the developed countries (in the range of 3 to 5 percent of disposable personal income, compared with 12 to 16 percent in Japan and 7 to 10 percent in Western Europe).[1]

Frank Levy and Richard Michel note that the major economic story of the post–World War II era is the sudden break in the trend of 27 years (1946–1973) of income growth, followed by 13 years (1973–1986) of income stagnation.[2] The declining standard of living for American families forced more family members into the workplace. Levy has shown that aggregate profiles of family income mask a significant social trend: more and more families have had to have multiple wage earners to improve their standard of living since 1973.[3] The number of multiple-wage earner households appears to have reached a threshold, however, meaning that any increases in aggregate family income in the future will not be from a larger proportion of multiple-wage earner situations.

Americans have financed their consumption over the last 15 years through a combination of reduced savings and borrowing. At the same time the personal savings rate was declining, the federal government was "dissaving," as evidenced by the huge budget deficits that began to appear in 1982. The national savings rate (households, businesses, and government combined) fell from 16.9 percent of GNP in 1971–73 to 12.8 percent of GNP in 1985–87.[4] Over the same period, the nation's rate of investment declined from 16.7 percent of GNP to 15.8 percent of GNP.[5] The decline in rate of investment was less than the decline in national savings rate because a growing proportion of U.S. investment was financed by foreign capital. This huge foreign investment resulted in large part because of the large trade deficit. Between 1982 and 1992, the United States moved from being the largest creditor nation to being the largest debtor nation. To regain its national balance, the United States must decrease consumption and increase savings.

What are the implications of this macroeconomic snapshot for colleges and universities? William Nordhaus points out that the business cycle has little impact on colleges and universities, in part because the best institutions are not demand constrained.[6] Nonetheless, the large national debt has meant that interest rates have been high to attract investors. These high rates, in turn, have meant huge borrowing costs for higher education. The prime rate increased in 1994 for the first time since 1989; during that period, the rates on long-term debt decreased and provided an opportunity for institutions to refinance their debt and achieve considerable savings.

Education must be viewed as a capital investment. If the nation consumes less and saves more, and hence is in a position to allocate more of its resources to capital investment (physical and human), will higher education see some of these resources? Probably not. The U.S. already has a large investment in higher education: 3 percent of the GNP, compared with 1.7 percent in Japan, 0.7 percent in Germany, and 0.8 percent in France.[7] Even with this significant edge in higher education investment, the growth of the U.S. economy lagged the growth of other industrialized nations during the 1980s.

Current national trends in labor productivity are not mirrored at colleges and universities. For most of the twentieth century, productivity in the U.S. lagged the productivity of most industrialized nations; since the early 1990s, the U.S. has become a leader in productivity. In 1990, for example, with U.S. labor productivity indexed at 100, Japan was rated at 83 and Germany at 79.[8] Since 1991, labor productivity in the U.S. has been growing at an annual rate of 2.5 percent, better than twice the average rate between 1970 and 1990.[9]

U.S. gains in labor productivity have come from increased investments in new equipment and technologies and from significant restructuring—including "re-engineering"—of organizations and work processes. The same increases in labor productivity have not occurred in colleges and universities, in large part because teaching and research are so labor intensive. Television and other instructional media did not gain the widespread acceptance that was promised when they were introduced, but increased usage will come with recent innovations in communications and information transmission. Technological advances in communications have also made the computer a more powerful tool. The widespread availability and use of personal computers on most campuses means that computers will be more and more integrated into the curricula.

A number of colleges and universities have followed the lead of business to restructure the organization and work functions of support units. This effort has been made possible by an increasing reliance on information technology, especially for processing transactions in a "paperless" environment. The integration of databases has also increased the analytical capacity of campus administrators.

Cost containment will be a major objective for higher education in the foreseeable future, as it has become for businesses. It is important to note that vigorous restructuring in the 1990s is being pursued by companies—like Procter and Gamble—that are in sound financial condition as well as corporations—like IBM, AT&T, and DEC—whose financial fortunes have declined because of listless response in the face of stiff competition. All institutions of higher education, whether currently beset by budgetary problems or enjoying freedom from fiscal worries, must become more aggressive in attacking the problem of cost increases. Between the early 1980s and the early 1990s, costs in higher education rose 2.8 percent per year, faster than the CPI.[10] Costs at independent institutions are increasing more rapidly than costs at public institutions, despite higher salaries offered by the public sector.[11] Some of the escalation in costs can be traced to increased activity in the student services and administrative arenas, especially in response to increased demand for advising, athletic, and health services on the one hand and increased regulatory and environmental requirements on the other.

Higher education was a $146 billion business in 1990–91. Total expenditures for higher education increased from 2.6 percent of the gross domestic product in 1980 to 2.9 percent in 1991.[12] Higher education's share now exceeds that of agriculture, which in 1989 represented 2.4 percent of the gross domestic product. In fall 1991, more than 14.4 million individuals were enrolled in full-time and part-time degree programs. Off-campus extension, noncredit continuing education, and community service programs reached many millions more. Academic programs available to adult learners are now ubiquitous in higher education; 94 percent of all institutions enroll adult or nontraditional students. In 1991, colleges and universities employed approximately 2.5 million people: approximately 834,000 faculty, 144,000 executive management and administrative personnel, 588,000 other professionals, and 925,000 nonprofessional staff.

An enterprise as large as higher education is affected by the same economic and political pressures that affect other major social programs. Some of the most significant pressures are long-term: personnel costs, especially in such a labor-intensive industry; the costs of plant maintenance; the prices of purchased goods and services, especially specialty items such as books and journal subscriptions; the costs of complying with federal regulations and mandated social programs; and reduced federal aid and state support as policy makers seek to control deficits produced by the recession.

Personnel Costs

By far the largest portion of higher education costs is faculty and staff compensation. In 1990, salaries, wages, and benefits accounted for nearly 80 percent of educational and general expenditures (see figure 2.1).[13] The labor-intensive nature of higher education poses real problems for budget planners. The principal difficulty is that higher education, as a professional industry, is beset by slow gains in productivity. Increased productivity in higher education is defined as an increase in the value of services without a concomitant increase in costs to the consumer of those services. Some service industries such as banks and insurance companies have, through the introduction of computer technologies, increased their productivity so as to allow for significant increases in salaries and wages without raising the cost of services. In higher education, however, as in most professional industries, it is more difficult to increase productivity by introducing new technologies. A true gain in productivity requires that the quality of the service be at least maintained. Thus, larger classes will not increase an instructor's productivity if the instruction becomes less effective.

Howard Bowen notes that "faculty compensation is less than half the total outlays for personnel and only a quarter of all expenditures."[14] This computation uses as its base all institutional expenditures, including auxiliary enterprises. If one limits the base to educational and general expenditures, which exclude capital expenditures and auxiliary enterprises, faculty compensation generally ranges from 40 to 55 percent of expenditures. Thus, faculty compensation accounts for a significant portion of an institution's budget and represents the largest portion of total employee compensation.

Bowen also points to three characteristics that separate service industries from other sectors of the economy.[15] First, many service industries are based on an intellectual foundation requiring many employees to have exceptional skills that can be obtained only through years of rigorous training and experience. Second, these industries are tradition-bound in part because they are responsible for maintaining and furthering the intellectual and cultural values and development of this country. Third, most service industries require that their professionals be physically present to their clients. This requirement for personal communication in the delivery of services places limits on the scale of operations. However, several

Figure 2.1   Percentage Allocation of Higher Education Costs, Education and General, FY 1990

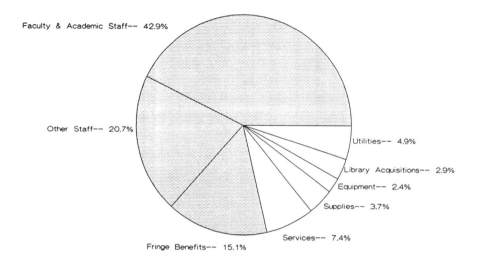

Faculty & Academic Staff-- 42.9%

Other Staff-- 20.7%

Utilities-- 4.9%

Library Acquisitions-- 2.9%

Equipment-- 2.4%

Supplies-- 3.7%

Services-- 7.4%

Fringe Benefits-- 15.1%

Source: Kent Halstead, *Higher Education Revenues & Expenditures, A Study of Institutional Costs* (Washington, DC: Research Associates of Washington, 1991)

The distribution of higher education subcomponent costs depicted for FY 1990 are based on extrapolations made by Kent Halstead using data originally collected for FY 1972. Halstead urges caution in interpreting the distribution in that additional subcomponents, not existing in 1972, may exist in current higher education budgets, or, an existing subcomponent may have taken on greater relative prominence. The proliferation of microcomputing on college campuses during this time period would be one example of a budgetary item not accounted for in 1972.

technologies that facilitate personal communication, including television, computers, and films, are available in higher education. Taking advantage of a gifted lecturer through telecasts or employing computer-assisted learning may represent a true increase in productivity.

Because such a large proportion of the costs in a labor-intensive industry are personnel related, the only way to achieve significant economies through nontechnological means is to control expenditures for salaries and wages. These economics usually require that, in the face of steady or declining budgets, salaries and wages or the number of employees be reduced. Colleges and universities that anticipate financial difficulties and plan accordingly probably will have more options available and have less traumatic experiences than institutions that do not have a firm grasp of their financial condition (see chapter 4). Cutting faculty and staff can sharply reduce morale if it is done over a very short period of time. Also, rapid reductions are difficult to accomplish without major distortions because of tenure and longer-term contracts. Allowing attrition through resignation, retirement, and death is perhaps the most humane form of action, but this strategy will not suffice for many institutions in the 1990s and beyond. Faculty and staff mobility probably will be limited during the next decade because many institutions will downsize in response to unfavorable economic conditions. However, retirements over the next decade probably will increase; 45 to 50 percent of the current faculty are 50 years or older.[16]

The relationship of the CPI to faculty and staff salaries and economic projections indicates that faculty and staff compensation policies will be a major consideration of budgeters during the next decade. As shown in figure 2.2, faculty salaries declined when measured in constant dollars between 1970 and 1990. Moreover, faculty salaries have lost ground to salaries in other professions in industry and government.

Even in the short run, it will be difficult for higher education to attract young people who are also in demand in industry and government and to retain the most able individuals in all fields. In the long term, if the overall quality of faculty and staff is to be maintained, the gap between academic and nonacademic salaries must be closed through some combination of a decrease in the supply of entrants competing for positions and an increase in demand. This may necessitate some hard choices. Across-the-board salary increases help maintain the real income of the entire group; but at the same time, when funds are not available to meet the market for those who are in demand, the quality of the faculty and staff suffers.

Costs of Plant Maintenance

Most colleges and universities enlarged their physical plants to accommodate increased student enrollments during the 1960s, 1970s, and

Figure 2.2 Faculty Pay and the Cost of Living

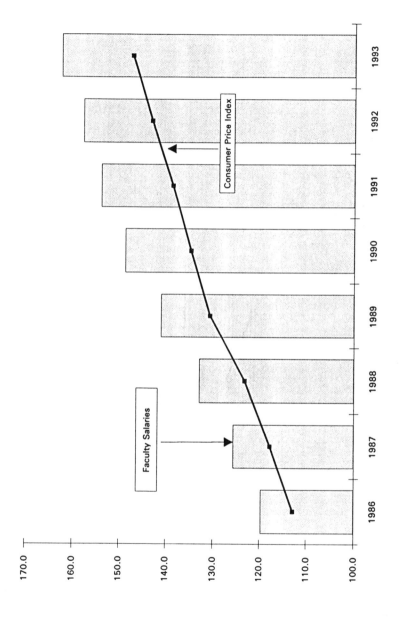

Source: American Association of University Professors; U.S. Dept. of Labor appearing in *The Chronicle of Higher Education,* April 14, 1993 Vol. XXXIX, No. 32 and April 20, 1994 Vol. XL, No. 33.

1980s. Because these facilities were new or recently renovated, they did not require significant expenditures for maintenance at the time. However, many of these facilities are now requiring substantial investments for upkeep as major building systems begin to wear out. Unfortunately, many institutional budgeters have become accustomed to allocating an insufficient share of budgets to plant maintenance, and the demand for increased maintenance expenditures is straining institutional budgets. Part of the shock comes from the inflated cost of replacement systems and renovation construction.

The vastness of the facilities problem cannot be overemphasized. One-third of higher education's physical plant is 30 or more years old; almost two-thirds is 20 or more years old. In 1989, the capital renewal and replacement needs of U.S. colleges and universities were estimated to be $60 billion; priority repairs and renovations, all urgent, required an estimated $20.5 billion of the $60 billion total.[17]

Even institutions that did not make major additions to their physical plants tend to balance budgets by skimping on plant maintenance. Facilities that are not regularly and adequately cared for deteriorate more quickly than those that are maintained. Many institutions, especially those in the public sector, not only defer maintenance for too long but also do not set aside a portion of annual operating expenses to create a reserve for depreciation. By not adequately anticipating the future costs of depreciation and obsolescence, budgeters leave their institutions vulnerable to shocks when suddenly unavoidable renovation costs beyond ordinary maintenance are incurred. Ideally, 1 to 3 percent of an institution's budget should be reserved for equipment and facilities maintenance.[18]

Prices of Purchased Goods and Services

To measure the average changes in prices for a "market basket" (fixed in terms of amount and quality) of goods and services purchased by colleges and universities through current fund educational and general expenditures, the Higher Education Price Index (HEPI) was developed. Updated annually, the HEPI is based on the salaries of faculty and staff; the prices for contracted services such as data processing, communications, and transportation; and the prices for supplies and materials, equipment, books and periodicals, and utilities. The various items are weighted in the HEPI according to their relative importance in an institution's current fund educational and general budget (excluding sponsored research), as estimated from national averages.

The prices of goods and services that colleges and universities buy have increased faster than the general price level in the economy since the early 1980s. The HEPI rose from 263.9 in 1981 to 377.6 in 1987 (1967=100), compared to an increase in the U.S. Bureau of Labor Statistics Producer Price Index (formerly called the Wholesale Price Index) from 269.8 to 295.7 during the same period.[19] Similarly, the ratio of the HEPI to the CPI increased from 0.992 in 1980–81 to 1.109 in 1989–90.[20]

Comparing the HEPI and the Producer Price Index hides some of the effects of inflation on colleges and universities. In many cases, higher education institutions have met rapid increases in the cost of utilities, books and periodicals, supplies, and employee benefits by holding down salary increases or eliminating faculty and staff positions. For example, although energy costs have quadrupled since the 1973 OPEC oil embargo, they are still a relatively small part of an institution's total operating budget when compared with faculty and staff salary costs (see figure 2.1). Growth in the costs of energy are driven more by consumption than by rate increases. Some colleges and universities have been able to balance projected utility bills with only minor restrictions on salary increases. But if this practice continues, the salary structure at those institutions will be seriously eroded.

Most institutional budgets cannot withstand major fluctuations caused by enormous jumps in the prices of goods and services. For example, the recent phenomenal increase in the cost of scholarly journals has forced many libraries to cancel subscriptions. Many reductions can be achieved at little or no cost, but marked reductions in fuel bills, for example, often can be realized only through major renovations that enhance energy efficiency or through the use of computers to monitor and control utility consumption. For many institutions, the cost of major energy conservation plans exceeds the amount of capital funds available to make the modifications.

Major increases in expenditures have occurred in noneducational and general activities, auxiliary enterprises, and hospitals, activities not reflected in the HEPI.[21] Colleges and universities continue to face the cost of replacing expensive instructional and research equipment purchased during the expansion of the past several decades. Unless institutions have set aside depreciation reserves with which to purchase replacement equipment, the purchases will have to be made from the current operating budget. Most institutional budgets cannot readily absorb the shock of such expenditures.

Perhaps the most stunning increases in costs have occurred in the benefits arena, especially in costs for health services for employees and retirees. Many institutions can no longer cover the full cost of health insurance, and are asking employees and retirees to assume an increasing share of the expenses. To control the cost of retirement programs, many colleges and universities are shifting from defined benefits programs, for which benefits are fixed on the basis of salary, age, and time of service, to defined contribution programs, for which the contribution is fixed but the payout at retirement depends upon the condition of the financial markets. In defined contribution plans, institutions often use 401(k) (cash or deferral) plans or 403(b) (tax-sheltered annuity) plans that encourage a contribution from the employee.

Costs of Federal Regulation and Social Programs

A portion of the costs of doing business in any industry can be attributed to informal social pressures and government mandates in a number of areas: personal security, work standards, personal opportunity, participation and due process, public information, and environmental protection.[22] Colleges and universities experience costs associated with these universal pressures and with several peculiar to higher education: emancipation of youth, federal grants and contracts, teaching hospitals and clinics, and tax reform. Federal regulations and mandated social programs touch all aspects of colleges and universities, from athletics to the care of laboratory animals.

It is difficult to isolate the fiscal impact of externally imposed regulations and guidelines. One reason is that colleges and universities may be sympathetic to the objectives of many of the programs and would want to implement the programs in some form on their own initiative. A second reason is that many of the costs of implementation cannot be separated from the routine operations of the institution.[23]

Several factors should be considered in assessing the impact of federal regulation and social pressures. First, the adoption of programs could result in increased or decreased costs. For example, a staff development program may lead to greater employee morale and productivity and hence decreased operating costs. Second, the costs of socially imposed programs should be considered in two parts: the costs of actual program operations, and the costs associated with compliance or the reporting of information. Much of the current concern about increases in institutional operating costs arises more from inefficiencies in how programs are implemented or information is provided than from actual operations. For example, administrators frequently complain that affirmative action reporting requirements are too detailed. Third, the costs of socially imposed programs should be analyzed over a specific period of time. Some programs require a one-time expenditure of large sums of money that, if amortized over time, would not be significant on an annual basis. Fourth, the implementation of some social programs may not lead to higher aggregate expenditures but to a redistribution of expenditures among the various activities included in the budget. The net effect is a reduction in the priority of some activities and thus in the amount of funding for them. For example, resources once earmarked for additional library acquisitions might be directed to implementing affirmative action programs.

Overall, profit-making enterprises probably have an advantage in dealing with socially imposed costs. In the for-profit sector, it is easier to pass on the costs of implementing these programs to the consumer through higher prices. However, colleges and universities must rely on additional funding from legislatures and donors and increases in tuition and fees. (Legislatures are sometimes sympathetic to the fact that public institutions incur additional costs in implementing programs but may be unwilling to increase taxes or cut other programs to compensate.) Increased costs that cannot be supported from these sources must be absorbed in the form of reduced instructional, research, and service programs.

Some of the specific mandates and requirements of the various social programs are summarized below to provide a sense of their complexity.

Personal security. Federal regulations and laws include the Social Security Act of 1935, as amended (retirement pensions, survivors' insurance, disability insurance, unemployment compensation, health insurance); the Occupational Safety and Health Act of 1970 (OSHA); the Employment Retirement Income Security Act of 1974 (ERISA); and legislation on radiation safety and the protection of human and animal subjects used in research and teaching.

Work standards. The major pieces of legislation are the National Labor Relations Act of 1935, which covers the rules of collective bargaining and employee organization; the Fair Labor Standards Act of 1938, which establishes minimum wages, maximum work hours, and overtime compensation; and the Equal Pay Act of 1963, which requires that employees doing similar work must receive equal pay regardless of the employee's sex.

Personal opportunity. In the area of affirmative action, federal regulations and laws include Executive Order 11246 of 1965, as amended in 1967, which prohibits discrimination on the basis of sex; the Employment Act of 1967, which prohibits discrimination on the basis of age; Title VII of the Civil Rights Act of 1964, as amended by the Equal Employment Opportunity Act of 1972, which prohibits discrimination on the basis of sex, race, creed, or national origin; Title IX of the Educational Amendments of 1972, which prohibits discrimination on the basis of sex in educational policies, facilities, programs, and employment practices; student financial aid program rules, some of which require institutional contributions or impose significant administrative burdens; Internal Revenue Service regulations concerning discrimination in employment and student admissions; and various judicial decisions.

Participation, openness, due process, and privacy. The guiding legislation includes the First Amendment of the Constitution; the National Labor Relations Act of 1935; and the Family Educational Rights and Privacy Act of 1974 (the Buckley Amendment), which deals with the management of records and the release of information.

Public information. Requests for information occur primarily in five areas: consumer protection, fund raising, enforcement of government programs, general statistical needs of society, and general public demands for accountability. Examples include the need to clear with the Office of Management and Budget (OMB) questionnaires on federal grants; the financial, faculty effort, and staff effort reporting requirements of OMB Circular A-21, which dictates the procedures for reporting the indirect costs incurred by research activities; audit reports on student aid; and the annual data reporting requirements of the Integrated Postsecondary Education Data System (IPEDS).

Environmental protection. Colleges and universities are increasingly affected by pollution control requirements, restrictions on research involving radiation or recombinant DNA, and, especially in urban settings, regulations on crime, vandalism, and the problems of neighborhood deterioration.

Disabilities. The Americans with Disabilities Act of 1990 specifies requirements for making programs and facilities accessible to persons with disabilities.

Emancipation of youth. The constitutional amendment lowering the age of majority to 18 had a visible impact in three areas: it altered significantly the nature of student services such as residence and dining facilities; greater demands are placed on student aid programs because more students declare themselves "independent" of their families and are less dependent on their families for financial support; and in-state and out-of-state student tuition and student aid differentials in the public sector are undermined when emancipated students establish residence where they attend college.

Shared costs in federal grants and contracts. Colleges and universities tend to absorb some of the costs associated with conducting research generated by federal grants and contracts in that overhead reimbursement generally does not cover all indirect costs associated with conducting research and certain granting agencies specifically require the sharing of direct costs. With the disclosure of irregularities in the reporting of indirect costs at Stanford University and several other institutions in the late 1980s and early 1990s, and in an effort to control the growth of the federal budget, the federal government is becoming more strict about what activities can be reimbursed. For example, the federal government recently limited staff support that can be charged as a direct expense of research. Now most support staff are considered to be covered as an indirect expense. The federal government is also considering a temporary ceiling on the total indirect cost reimbursement that an institution can charge.

Special costs of teaching hospitals and clinics. Teaching hospitals and clinics are subject to restrictions and guidelines governing patient care review, accreditation and licensure, accounting procedures, use of drugs and blood, use of radiation, and use of human and animal subjects for research. National health care reform could seriously undermine the nation's medical schools and teaching medical centers unless the costs of medical instruction are reorganized.

Tax reform. The Internal Revenue Code of 1986 had significant implications for higher education, many of them negative. Although tax brackets were eliminated and tax rates were reduced, many deductions and means to shift income were eliminated, leading to an increased cost of education for many citizens. Subsequent changes to the code reintroduced the advantages of contributions. Large independent institutions face restrictions on tax-exempt debt financing: all 501(c)(3) organizations—educational, scientific, charitable, and religious organizations—are individually limited to $150 million of outstanding tax-exempt bonds. The code also set new limits on existing 401(k) and 403(b) deferred compensation plans.[24]

The Size of the Traditional College-Age Population

The demographic profile of the United States will profoundly affect higher education institutions in the coming years. The number of individuals in the traditional college-age population (18–24 years old) declined from 30 million in 1979–80 to an estimated 26.4 million in 1990–91. By 2002–03, the number of 18–24 years old is expected to increase to 27.3 million.

Changing demographics will affect different regions and types of institutions differently. It is also important to distinguish between demographic data, which reflect existing conditions, and enrollment projections, which are based on assumptions of high school graduation rates, college attendance rates, student loan policies, and labor market conditions.

As a result of the changing demographic profile, most colleges and universities will engage in intense competition for students during the next decade. Institutions should expect their advertising, promotional, and recruiting costs to increase markedly. To be more attractive to potential students, institutions will probably have to offer more financial aid. Academic programs for which there is strong student demand will have to be expanded, and some academic programs will have to be changed to become more attractive. Offerings will have to be scheduled at convenient times and locations to accommodate adult learners. Public institutions may have to seek a larger proportion of out-of-state students.

Changes in Federal Funding Philosophy

The manner in which the federal government funds social programs in general, and higher education in particular, will greatly affect the revenues of colleges and universities during the next decade. Fewer federal dollars will be directed toward higher education because of deep-rooted changes in funding philosophy and growing competition from other sectors of government. In addition, the size of the national debt continues to nag national policy makers.

The reexamination of the federal role in higher education raises the questions of who benefits from and who should pay for higher education. More and more policy makers believe that the balance of benefits has shifted from society to the individual. Some of these policy makers have come to believe that the current system of higher education is overbuilt. A major aspect of the debate over who should pay for higher education is determining the proper balance between federal, state, and local governments.

Before World War II, states were largely responsible for public subsidies to public higher education in the form of low tuition. Few public funds were directed to independent institutions in the form of institutional aid. After World War II, the federal government became a more important participant in financing higher education. The G.I. Bill of Rights of 1944 provided massive sums of money to institutions as well as to students. Both public and independent institutions benefitted from this law. The balance was altered, however, in the early 1950s when the Korean conflict G.I. Bill awarded funds for college directly to veterans without awarding institutional aid. The federal government broadened its support of higher education in 1958 with the National Defense Education Act. This law provided funds to institutions as well as to students, especially students at the graduate level. During the late 1950s and 1960s, the federal government provided considerable funds for buildings and facilities, libraries, and research and training. Direct aid to institutions peaked in 1965–66 and declined thereafter as federal involvement in higher education began to focus on student aid. The 1972 Amendments to the Higher Education Act of 1965 established the policy of basing federal student assistance programs on need.[25]

Federal money awarded in the form of grants and contracts for research development and training are of the same order of magnitude as student aid funding. The federal government has attempted to maintain a delicate balance between funding the public sector and funding the independent sector by avowedly favoring neither.

A reevaluation of the federal government's role in supporting higher education began in the early 1980s. (An example is the removal of educational survivor benefits from Social Security.) During the previous three decades the nation's focus had moved from mass to universal higher education. The philosophy guiding federal support for this transition was based on increasing access to higher education by promoting student aid. Over this period, the emphasis on aid to economically disadvantaged individuals was broadened to include the middle class.

Higher education's role as the primary means of social mobility has been the foundation of federal support of higher education. Over the last 30 years, however, the character of higher education has changed markedly. The community college movement, for example, greatly expanded access to some form of college experience. College student bodies are no longer composed exclusively of full-time students in the 18-to-21 age group. More part-time students and adult learners are seeking college training while they support families and maintain jobs. More individuals are returning to college for recertification or to upgrade their professional skills or to embark on training for new careers.

The new relationship between the federal government and higher education will probably shift the burden of support away from the federal level. States and individual consumers of higher education will likely be asked to bear more of the costs. One example is the shift from grants to loans for financial aid. Another is the increasing attention being given to community service as a way to reimburse loans. Business and industry and nonprofit research organizations may also be expected to take on more of the burden of basic and applied research.

State and Local Factors

State and local governments are the single most important source of financial support of higher education in the United States. Of the $149.8 billion in current funds received by all public and independent colleges and universities in fiscal year (FY) 1991, $43 billion (29 percent) came from state and local government appropriations and grants and contracts. Other major revenue sources were tuition and fees ($37.4 billion—25 percent) and federal appropriations and grants and contracts ($18.2 billion—12.2 percent). The remainder came from auxiliary enterprises, institutional sources such as endowment income and sales and services of educational activities, and private gifts.[26]

State and local economic and political factors have a significant impact on the fiscal fortunes of individual institutions. For example, the cost of energy and labor is generally cheaper in the Sunbelt than in the Northeast. The cost of housing is generally higher in metropolitan areas than in rural areas and becomes a factor in establishing the salary structure for faculty and staff and the housing rates for students. State and local regulations often mirror federal programs in areas such as workers' compensation, building and safety codes, public health standards, occupational health and safety programs, unemployment compensation, and retirement programs.

Perhaps the most systematic way to approach the differences in state and local environments is to examine the level of state wealth, the willingness of state and local governments to tax that wealth, and the proportion of the taxes that state and local governments are willing to direct to higher education.

The level of economic activity in a state and the sum of personal wealth contribute to state wealth. This is measured as tax capacity, which is an index of the potential to obtain revenues for public purposes through various kinds of taxes. Marilyn McCoy and D. Kent Halstead define the tax capacity of a state and its local governments as the amount of revenue they could raise (relative to other state and local governments) if all 50 state-local government systems applied tax rates at the national average to their respective tax bases.[27] The tax base is shaped by a state's demographic profile and the economic mix of manufacturing, agriculture, and service industries. In FY 1985, values in relative tax capacity ranged from $3,648 per capita in Alaska (159 percent above the national average) to

$972 per capita in Mississippi (31 percent below the national average).[28] Thus, Mississippi had only 27 percent of the inherent tax wealth of Alaska from which to support public services in FY 1985.

The willingness of state and local governments to tax their wealth is measured by tax effort, or the revenues collected as a percentage of state and local tax capacity. In FY 1985, New York demonstrated the greatest tax effort (with an index 56 percent above the national average), and Nevada the smallest (with an index 64 percent below the national average).[29] This means that New York demanded more of its tax capacity in that year than did Nevada.

Collected tax revenues represent the funds available to state and local governments and are a product of tax capacity and tax effort. A state with low tax capacity and high tax effort can collect an average amount of tax revenues. Virginia, for example, collected revenues of $1,376 per capita in FY 1985 (compared to a national average of $1,408) on the basis of a tax capacity that ranked 24th nationally (2 percent below the national average) and a tax effort that ranked 37th nationally (13 percent below the national average).[30]

Several factors determine the proportion of state and local government revenues appropriated for higher education. Commitment to social programs varies widely among the states. Generally, the stronger the competition for resources in a state, the smaller the share allocated to any one social service. During the 1980s, the priority of higher education on states' lists of social services declined. There is every indication that higher education's ranking will not improve during the 1990s; in fact, it seems likely that the demand for support of prisons, health care, and welfare systems will increase significantly, further displacing higher education. Moreover, as state and local governments are asked to carry more of the cost of social services currently funded by the federal government, lower-priority services such as higher education will receive smaller shares of state and local resources.

Another determinant of appropriations is the nature of the higher education system in a state. A system composed of many community colleges is probably considerably less expensive to operate than one with a similar number of institutions but with more at the four-year level or above. Some states, particularly those in the Northeast, traditionally have a very strong independent sector and depend on those institutions to enroll a large number of students who might otherwise attend public institutions. A few states, such as New Jersey, experience a considerable outmigration of potential students and allocate relatively fewer resources to higher education. Some states, such as Maryland, base their contributions to the independent sector on the level of support for public colleges and universities.

Sources of Funds

Colleges and universities in both the public and independent sectors rely on a variety of sources for financial support. Although the sources are similar from one institution to another, the extent to which any one source is tapped depends on the institution's character. Thus, independent institutions usually rely more on student tuition and fees than do public institutions. Large research-oriented universities in both the public and the independent sectors receive a greater proportion of their support from government grants and contracts than do four-year public and independent colleges. This contract and grant money is restricted to specific scholarly programs, however, and cannot be used for general support.

Figure 2.3 presents each of the revenue types. For each type of revenue, the aspects common to public and independent institutions are presented first; features peculiar to the sectors are presented separately. The figure does not identify student aid as a source of institutional revenue because it flows into the institution indirectly through students. However, as noted earlier, federal and state support for higher education via student aid is considerable. (The impact of student aid as an indirect source of revenue is discussed as part of tuition and fees.) Figure 2.4 summarizes the proportions of income from the several sources of revenue.

Tuition and Fees

Tuition is the price of an instructional service rendered to students, but unlike most prices it represents only a portion of the costs incurred in providing the service. Some of the factors considered in the setting of tuition levels are:

☐   tuition at peer institutions;
☐   the need to balance the budget;

Figure 2.3   Institutional Resources

Source	Type of Revenue	Received Through
Students	Tuition and fees	Charge to customer
Government		
Federal	Appropriations Grants and contracts —Direct costs —Indirect costs	Subsidy Reimbursement for services
State and local	Appropriations Grants and contracts —Direct costs —Indirect costs	Subsidy Reimbursement for services
Private (individual or corporate)	Gifts Grants and contracts —Direct costs —Indirect costs Contributed services	Contribution Reimbursement for services Subsidy
Institutional endowment and fund balances	Investment earnings	Investment of working capital and permanent funds
Sales and services	Educational activities Auxiliary enterprises Medical services	Charge to customer Charge to customer Charge to customer

Source: *Financial Responsibilities of Governing Boards of Colleges and Universities* (Washington: AGB and NACUBO, 1979), p. 20.

☐   student financial aid needs;
☐   tradition or philosophy of the institution or the state system; and
☐   general economic conditions.

"Price setting" is a very important budget decision that requires an understanding of the institution's market position and the elasticity of student demand. Demand elasticity dictates that when prices are higher

Figure 2.4 Sources of Current Funds Revenues for Institutions of Higher Education by Control And Level of Institution, Fiscal Year 1990–91

Source	Total All Institutions	Public Institutions		Independent Institutions	
		Four-Year	Two-Year	Four Year	Two Year
		Amount in Millions			
Government	$ 59.244	$38.445	$11.043	$ 9.646	$ 110
Federal	17.255	8.469	702	8.021	62
State	38.349	29.540	7.513	1.252	45
Local	3.640	436	2.828	373	2
Private Sources	7.781	3.249	119	4.345	67
Students	47.865	18.574	3.720	24.537	1.034
Tuition and Fees	33.926	11.090	2.730	19.213	893
Aux. Enterprises	13.938	7.484	990	5.324	141
Institutional	24.746	13.148	613	10.914	70
Total	$139.635	$73.416	$15.496	$49.443	$1.281
	Percentage Distribution				
Government	42.4%	52.4%	71.3%	19.5%	8.6%
Federal	12.4	11.5	4.5	16.2	4.9
State	27.5	40.2	48.5	2.5	3.5
Local	2.6	0.6	18.3	0.8	0.2
Private Sources	5.6	4.4	0.8	8.8	5.3
Students	34.3	25.3	24.0	49.6	80.7
Tuition and Fees	24.3	15.1	17.6	38.9	69.7
Aux. Enterprises	10.0	10.2	6.4	10.8	11.0
Institutional	17.7	17.9	4.0	22.1	5.5
Total	100.0%	100.0%	100.0%	100.0%	100.0%

Source: U.S. Department of Education, National Center for Education Statistics, Integrated Postsecondary Education Data System (IPEDS) Finance Survey.

fewer students seek admission than when prices are lower. Some institutions, such as the Ivy League universities, need not be so concerned about reduced demand when they raise charges because they already turn away well-qualified students. Colleges and universities with a regional audience, on the other hand, may find that they are much more restricted in setting tuition if they wish to maintain or increase enrollment levels.

To remain competitive, institutions must be sensitive to their peers' net student charges (tuition charges less financial assistance). During the Bush Administration, the Justice Department charged Ivy League universities and several other selective independent institutions with collusion in the sharing of financial aid data for prospective students. MIT challenged the federal government in court and won for institutions the right to share aggregate financial aid information.

In comparing peer institutions, the presumed quality of education provided by each and the effect of the net price on enrollment must be considered. Tuition levels are often determined by the amount of income needed to balance the budget within the constraints of institutional philosophy and market position. This factor is closely related to the economic climate at the time the budget is prepared. When costs increase rapidly, tuition will also rise markedly. However, the institution must weigh the ability and willingness of prospective students to pay higher tuition. Some institutions have strong traditions that govern the setting of tuition levels. For example, the California system of public higher education for many years had a policy of no tuition and low student fees. During California's economic difficulties in the early 1990s, this policy had to be abandoned as fee charges were increased markedly to provide revenues to compensate for the loss of state appropriations.

Other institutions seek to set tuition at a fixed percentage of the estimated annual cost of education. This policy was used by the state of Virginia for many years, until the economic downturn of the early 1990s. When state appropriations failed to keep pace with the growth of institutional costs, tuition rates had to be increased to the point that the revenue exceeded the agreed-to proportion of the annual cost of education.

Fees for special activities or purposes tend to be based as closely as possible on the actual costs of services. Examples of activities or services for which fees are charged include intercollegiate athletics, laboratory usage or breakage, instructional materials, health insurance or health services, student organizations, and debt service.

For student aid, the setting of tuition levels has a significant effect on the expenditure side of the revenue equation. Institutions with a strong commitment to student aid, such as those that provide considerable aid from their own funds, must usually plan to increase their aid expenditures to parallel the increase in tuition so as not to price themselves out of their traditional student markets. Institutional student aid also becomes more important in the face of reductions in federal student aid.

Independent institutions. Tuition and fee income in FY 1990 represented 38.9 percent of all current fund income at four-year independent institutions and 69.7 percent of all income at two-year independent colleges.[31]

Because tuition and fee income represents a much greater proportion of institutional income for the private sector than for the public sector, balancing the budget through tuition increases is a primary consideration for independent institutions. Thus, the rate of tuition increases at independent institutions is typically related, under steady-state conditions, to the CPI, the HEPI, and family income.

Public institutions. Tuition and fee income in FY 1990 represented 15.1 percent of all income at four-year public institutions and 17.6 percent at two-year public colleges.[32]

Setting tuition in the public sector is often more complicated and indirect than in the private sector. James Rusk and Larry Leslie argue that adjusting state appropriations seems to be the major way to influence tuition levels.[33] They also explain that tuition increases are higher where state effort is insufficient to satisfy the financial needs of the institutions. Similarly, in states that have a substantial proportion of their enrollments in independent institutions, the public colleges and universities have tuition rates much higher than the average. The reverse is also true.

The policies and procedures for setting tuition and student fees in public institutions vary widely across states. Charles L. Length summarizes the underlying philosophies, as presented in figure 2.5. He presents the economic and cost factors used to set tuition and fees in figure 2.6.[34]

It should be noted that in some states tuition and fee income is part of the legislative appropriation, while in others it is treated inde-

Figure 2.5 Variations in Tuition Philosophy And Procedures

	Number of States		
Philosophy	Research Universities	State colleges and universities	Community Colleges
Low tuition philosophy	8 (16%)	6 (12%)	14 (29%)
Moderate tuition philosophy	18 (30%)	21 (44%)	19 (40%)
High tuition policy	5 (10%)	5 (10%)	3 (6%)
Tuition "indexed" to comparable institutions	7 (14%)	6 (12%)	4 (8%)
Institution-level decisions only	12 (24%)	10 (21%)	8 (17%)
Total	50	48	48

Figure 2.6 Economic and Cost Factors Used in Setting Tuition

	Number of States		
Factor	Indexed	Indirect	No Explicit or Implicit recognition
Consumer Price Index (CPI)	2	23	19
Higher Education Price Index (HEPI)	3	17	26
State personal income or disposable income	1	20	25
Cost of education or instructional costs	10	27	10
Peer group interinstitutional comparisons	6	32	9
State general fund appropriations for higher education	8	31	9

Note: Typically, more than one economic or cost factor is taken into account in setting tuition levels, particularly when the relationship is indirect.

pendently as an institutional revenue fund and therefore does not appear in the appropriations bill. Generally, institutions have more flexibility in the use of funds if those funds do not appear in the appropriations bill.

Federal Student Aid Programs

The American Council on Education prepared the following summary of federal student assistance programs. The numbers cited are illustrative only, because federal laws and regulations often change. In fall 1985, 58.3 percent of full-time undergraduate students received some form of financial aid (47.4 percent received financial aid from the federal government); in fall 1989, 56.4 percent of full-time undergraduate students received some form of financial aid (41.9 percent received financial aid from the federal government).[35]

Pell Grants. The Higher Education Act of 1972 established the Basic Education Opportunity Grants Program, now called the Federal Pell Grant Program, to provide students with a minimum level of assistance that could be used at any postsecondary institution. Although the institution disburses the funds, the individual student's eligibility is determined by national needs analysis.

The needs analysis system functions as a means test to reduce awards as family income increases. Actual awards are limited by appropriations (a reduction formula applies when funds are insufficient) and by a provision limiting grants to no more than one-half the cost of attendance. In FY 1992, Congress appropriated $5.242 billion, providing 4 million awards averaging $1,302 each.

Campus-based programs. Educational Opportunity Grants, now called Federal Supplemental Educational Opportunity Grants, were established by the Higher Education Act of 1965 to provide federal grants for needy students as selected by the institution. Funds are distributed to institutions according to a state allocation formula based on proportionate undergraduate enrollments. In FY 1992, Congress appropriated $415 million, providing 728,000 grants averaging $570 each to needy students.

The Federal Work-Study Program was established by the Economic Opportunity Act of 1964. The federal government provides 80 percent of funds to pay wages of needy students employed by colleges, universities, or nonprofit agencies. Funds are distributed to institutions according to a state allocation formula based on that state's proportion of higher education enrollments, high school graduates, and children in poverty-level families. Institutions put up 20 percent, and they select the recipients. In FY 1992, Congress appropriated $791 million, which provided 841,000 grants averaging $940 each.

The National Defense Student Loan program, now called the Federal Perkins Loan Program, established by the National Defense Education Act of 1958, provides low-interest loans for needy students. The federal government provides 90 percent of the capital. Funds are distributed directly to institutions under a state allocation formula based on proportionate enrollments in higher education. Institutions select and contribute 10 percent and collect the principal and interest paid on previous loans to be recycled for new borrowers. In FY 1992, Congress appropriated $824 million in new federal loan capital, which provided 660,000 awards averaging $1,248 each.

Federal State Student Incentive Grants. The Higher Education Act of 1972 also established State Student Incentive Grants (SSIG) to encourage the creation of state scholarship programs for needy students. States match federal grants and allocate them to institutions. In FY 1992, Congress appropriated $60 million, providing awards to 240,000 students.

Federal Family Education Loan Program (FFELP). The Higher Education Act of 1965 established the Guaranteed Student Loan program, now called the Federal Family Education Loan Program. The program insures loans made by private lenders to students and reinsures loans guaranteed by state or private nonprofit agencies, subsidizes in-school interest for students up to a specified income level, and pays a special allowance to the lender to make up the difference between the student interest rate and market rates. The program is an entitlement, with annual costs to be met by the Treasury based on the dollar volume of outstanding loans, money market conditions, and the default rate. The term FFELP now encompasses several student loan programs. In FY 1992, 3.85 million Federal Stafford Student Loans were made totaling $10.6 billion, and 670,000 Supplemental Loans for Students (SLS) were made totaling $1.95 billion. (The SLS program ended on July 1, 1994.)

The Education Amendments of 1980 established the parent loan program as part of the FFELP. This program was expanded in 1981 to include graduate and professional students and independent students. The Federal Parent Loans for Undergraduate Students program does not subsidize in-school interest, but the federal government pays a special allowance to lenders to make up the difference between the borrower's interest rate and market rates. Full-time students may defer principal payments but not interest; other students must pay principal and interest in regular installments beginning 60 days after origination. In FY 1992, 348,000 recipients were awarded $1.125 billion under this program.

The first loans under the Federal Direct Student Loan Program were issued on July 1, 1994. The program, authorized under the Student Loan Reform Act of 1993, allows the federal government to provide loan capital directly to student and parent borrowers through institutions.

State Student Aid Programs

Most states have scholarship programs for needy students. State funds for these programs match federal money provided as Federal State Student Incentive Grants. The support for scholarship programs far exceeds the federal contribution in several states. Some states also have competitive as well as need-based programs. Because the character of higher education in individual states varies considerably, state aid programs also differ widely. Most state student aid programs have maximum awards, with the limit set at tuition or a dollar ceiling. Awards are also made to students who attend out-of-state institutions in some programs.

Government Sources of Funding

Public and independent institutions receive funding from the federal government and from state and local governments in the form of direct appropriations and contracts and grants. Contracts and grants are awarded on a competitive basis, and the federal government does not differentiate between public and independent institutions. There are usually two parts to a grant or contract: direct costs and indirect costs. Direct costs represent the award to the institution for conducting the actual research or project. The award is restricted in that it can be expended only for the research activity. Included in direct costs are the salary costs of the investigators, graduate assistants, and support staff; and funds for supplies, equipment, and operating costs associated with the research or activity. Indirect costs are a reimbursement to the institution for overhead costs associated with conducting research activities. Indirect costs are generally computed as a percentage of direct costs and include charges for utilities, facilities maintenance, library usage, and the administrative costs of processing research proposals, monitoring the expenditure of contract and grant funds, and complying with reporting requirements.

The federal government makes appropriations directly to public and independent institutions in the form of categorical support for college libraries, library research and training, veterans' costs of instruction, cooperative education, law school clinical experience, land-grant aid, women's educational equity programs, support of developing institutions, international education, and vocational education.

Independent institutions. Income from federal sources, including appropriations and restricted and unrestricted grants and contracts, represented 16.2 percent of all current fund income in four-year independent institutions and 4.9 percent in two-year colleges in 1989–90. Appropriations and grants and contracts income from state and local governments represented 3.8 percent of all income in four-year independent institutions and 3.7 percent in independent institutions in 1989–90.[36]

State and local appropriations to independent institutions take a number of forms. Approximately one-third of the states contract with independent colleges and universities for a wide variety of instructional services. Most of these arrangements involve the "purchase" of student spaces in special programs, such as health sciences.

About one-fifth of the states support the acquisition of new physical facilities at independent institutions through special state grants or by extending public authority to borrow funds through the sale of public bonds.[37]

Certain states provide direct support to independent institutions in the form of contracts based on the full-time equivalent enrollment of instate students, and others appropriate funds to independent colleges and universities for capitation grants. Under the Bundy Plan in New York, for example, the state bases aid on the number of degrees conferred at the bachelor's, master's, and doctoral levels.

Public institutions. Income from federal sources, including appropriations and restricted and unrestricted grants and contracts, represented 11.5 percent of all income in four-year public institutions and 4.5 percent in two-year public colleges in 1989–90. Appropriations and grants and contract income from state and local sources represented 40.8 percent of all income in four-year public institutions and 66.8 percent in public two-year colleges in 1989–90.[38]

State and local appropriations represent the single largest source of revenue to public institutions. These appropriations cover current operating expenses and capital construction costs.

Private Sources of Funding

Both public and independent institutions receive funds from private sources in the form of gifts, grants and contracts, and contributed services. Corporations, foundations, churches, alumni, local supporters, members of the institution's governing board, and friends provide these funds.

Independent institutions depend more heavily than public institutions on gifts for a substantial portion of each year's budget. Gifts are credited as current fund income to the extent that they are spent during the budget year. Gifts are designated as unrestricted or restricted. Unrestricted gifts allow an institution flexibility because they can be spent for any purpose. Restricted gifts are earmarked by the donor for specified activities. When the activities enhanced by restricted money are high on an institution's list of priorities, restricted funds can be used in place of institutional funds, thereby freeing the latter for other uses. Although institutions depend on gift support to varying degrees in their budget planning, this income is not always reliable. In years of economic downturn, for example, corporate giving often declines. In addition, philanthropic and corporate giving is sensitive to fluctuations in tax laws, and events on campus can have an important bearing on the level of giving by alumni or local supporters. If giving targets are not achieved, the institution must cut expenditures or draw on restricted funds.

Contracts and grants from private sources generally have direct and indirect cost components. The primary difference between contracts and grants from private sources and those from the government is that the indirect cost recovery rate applied to private contracts and grants is sometimes lower than the rate applied to government contracts and grants.

Some independent church-related colleges are subsidized through the contributed services of members of the religious order. The most significant contributions come in the form of teaching. In some colleges, the teaching members of the religious order receive salaries equal to those of lay members, and the order returns the salaries as a gift to the college.

Independent institutions. Revenues from private sources represented 8.8 percent of all income in four-year independent institutions and 5.3 percent of all income in two-year independent colleges in 1989–90.[39]

Public institutions. Revenues from private sources represented 4.4 percent of all income in four-year public institutions and 0.8 percent in two-year public colleges in 1989–90.[40]

Income from the Investment of Endowment And Fund Balances

Public and independent institutions often have funds available that can be invested for the purpose of generating income. These include endowment, current, loan, and life income and annuity funds. Endowments are permanent funds established to provide institutions with a regular source of investment income. The portfolio of investments is selected on the basis of both income-generating potential and the potential for long-term growth. A portion of the income earned from endowment fund investments is returned to the endowment so that the endowment can be maintained in real terms to provide a hedge against inflation. The size of institutional endowment funds varies widely. In 1993 Harvard University's endowment exceeded $5 billion, and the University of Texas System and Yale and Princeton universities had endowments in excess of $3 billion; only the 294 largest endowments were more than $35 million.[41] Thus, for the vast majority of institutions in the United States, endowment income is quite small.

The cash flow in most institutions is such that any surplus in the current operating fund is invested on a short-term basis. At the beginning of each semester, for example, when student tuition is usually paid, institutions tend to have more cash on hand than at other times of the year. The excess funds can be invested for the short term. For public institutions, rules governing short-term investment of institutional operating funds vary from state to state. Some states allot funds to institutions on a quarterly basis so that the state itself can invest its money and collect the income rather than allowing institutions to do so. Other states allot their appropriation at the beginning of the year and allow institutions the flexibility to invest the funds. Use of the earnings from the investment of fund balances may be restricted or unrestricted. For example, earnings on the investment of restricted student loan fund balances may be used only for student loans.

Independent institutions. Revenues from the investment of endowment and fund balances represented 5.2 percent of all income in independent institutions in 1990–91.[42]

Public institutions. Revenues from the investment of endowment and fund balances represented 0.5 percent of all income in public institutions in 1990–91.[43]

Income from Sales and Services

Colleges and universities receive income from the sale of educational and medical services and from auxiliary enterprises. Educational activities might include film rentals, testing services, home economics cafeterias, demonstration schools, dairy creameries, and college theaters.[44] Medical services are provided through teaching hospitals, student and staff health centers, and hearing and speech clinics. Auxiliary enterprises, which are generally self-supporting, include activities such as residence and dining halls, student unions, student bookstores, and intercollegiate athletics.

Independent institutions. Income from sales and services represented 23.0 percent of all income in independent institutions in FY 1991.[45]

Public institutions. Income from sales and services in FY 1991 represented 22.3 percent of all income in public institutions.[46]

For Further Reading

The literature on the economic and political environment runs from the journalistic to the deeply theoretical, with several regular compilations of national data in between. Examples of journalistic approaches include Carl Irving, "Stanford Gets New Ax Ready," *San Francisco Examiner*, November 24, 1991; Liz McMillen, "Yale U. Buffeted by Storm Over Its Fiscal Problems," *The Chronicle of Higher Education*, December 4, 1991, pp. A45-A46; Robert L. Jacobson, "Academic Leaders Predict Major Changes for Higher Education in Recession's Wake," *The Chronicle of Higher Education*, November 20, 1991, pp. A1, A35–A36; and Anthony DePalma, "With Deficit, Can Yale Still Be Great?" *The New York Times*, December 4, 1991, p. B7 (national edition).

Articles of more depth include Thomas W. Langfitt, "The Cost of Higher Education: Lessons to Learn from the Health Care Industry"; Robert Lemsky and William E. Massy, "Cost Containment: Committing to a New Economic Reality"; Catherine Gardner, Timothy R. Warner, and Rick Biedenweg, "Stanford and the Railroad: Case Studies of Cost Cutting"; and Kent John Chabotar and James P. Honan, "Coping with Retrenchment: Strategies and Tactics," all in *Change 22, no. 6* (November/December 1990). See also James Harvey, "Footing the Bill: Financial Prospects for Higher Education," *Educational Record 73, no. 4* (Fall 1992): 11–17; Eliot Marshall and Joseph Palca, "Cracks in the Ivory Tower," *Science 257* (August 28, 1992): 11961201; and Harold T. Shapiro, "The Fiscal Crisis and Higher Education: Current Realities and Future Prospects," *Academe 78, no. 7* (January/February 1993): 10–15.

The condition of physical facilities in higher education is discussed in Harvey H. Kaiser, "Rebuilding the Campus"; Walter A. Schaw, "The Time Bomb Continues to Tick"; Patricia Senn Breivik and Ward Shaw, "Libraries Prepare for an Information Age"; Ernest L. Boyer, "Buildings Reflect Our Priorities"; Jack Hug, "Research Facilities Needs Soar"; and Caspa L. Harris Jr. and David S. Byer, "Salvaging Tomorrow's Higher Education Facilities Today," all in *Educational Record 70, no. 1* (Winter 1989). See also John A. Dunn Jr., *Financial Planning Guidelines for Facility Renewal and Adaption* (Ann Arbor, MI: The Society for College and University Planning, 1989); Sean C. Rush and Sandra L. Johnson, *The Decaying American Campus: A Ticking Time Bomb* (Alexandria, VA: Association of Physical Plant Administrators of Universities and Colleges,

1989); and Harvey H. Kaiser, *Crumbling Academe* (Washington, DC: Association of Governing Boards, 1984).

Detailed analyses of economic conditions are found in Stephen A. Hoenack and Eileen L. Collins, eds., *The Economics of American Universities: Management, Operations, and Fiscal Environment* (Albany: State University of New York Press, 1990); William Becker and Darrell Lewis, eds., *The Economics of American Higher Education* (Norwell, MA: Kluwer, 1992); and William Becker and Darrell Lewis, eds., *Higher Education and Economic Growth* (Norwell, MA: Kluwer, 1993). The latter two volumes focus on the effects of higher education on the economic gains of individuals and the economic growth of society, respectively. See also Charles Clotfelder, Ronald Ehrenburg, Malcolm Getz, and John Siegfried, *Economic Challenges in Higher Education* (Chicago: University of Chicago Press, 1991), and Larry L. Leslie and Paul T. Brinkman, *The Economic Value of Higher Education* (New York: American Council on Education/Macmillan Publishing Company, 1988).

References that focus on higher education finance include Richard E. Anderson and Joel W. Meyerson, eds., *Financial Planning Under Economic Uncertainty*, New Directions for Higher Education no. 69 (San Francisco: Jossey-Bass Inc., 1990); Richard E. Anderson and Joel W. Meyerson, eds., *Financing Higher Education in a Global Economy* (New York: American Council on Education/Macmillan Publishing Company, 1990); and Richard E. Anderson and Joel W. Meyerson, eds., *Financing Higher Education: Strategies After Tax Reform*, New Directions for Higher Education no. 58 (San Francisco: Jossey-Bass Inc., 1987).

Useful compilations of data include the most recent edition of the annual volume compiled by the editors of *The Chronicle of Higher Education, The Almanac of Higher Education 1994* (Chicago: The University of Chicago Press, 1994); Kent Halstead, *State Profiles: Financing Public Higher Education 1978 to 1992* (Washington, DC: Research Associates of Washington, 1992); Kent Halstead, *Inflation Measures for Schools and Colleges: 1992 Update* (Washington, DC: Research Associates of Washington, 1992); Kent Halstead, *Higher Education Revenues & Expenditures: A Study of Institutional Costs* (Washington, DC: Research Associates of Washington, 1991); Edward R. Hines, *State Higher Education Appropriations 1992–93* (Denver: State Higher Education Executive Officers, 1993); and *Estimates of Fall 1992 Enrollment at Public, Four-Year Institutions* (Washington, DC: National Association of State Universities and Land-Grant Colleges and American Association of State Colleges and Universities, 1993).

Notes

1. Richard E. Anderson and Joel W. Meyerson, *Financing Higher Education in a Global Economy* (San Francisco: Jossey-Bass Inc., 1990), p. 15.
2. Frank S. Levy and Richard C. Michel, *The Economic Future of American Families: Income and Wealth Trends* (Washington, DC: The Urban Institute Press, 1991), p.3.
3. Frank Levy, *Dollars and Dreams: The Changing American Income Distribution* (New York: Russell Sage Foundation, 1987).
4. Levy and Michel, p. 2.
5. Ibid.
6. William Nordhaus, "Evaluating the Risks for Specific Institutions," in Richard E. Anderson and Joel W. Meyerson, eds., *Financial Planning Under Economic Uncertainty*, New Directions for Higher Education no. 69 (San Francisco: Jossey-Bass Inc., 1990).
7. Anderson and Meyerson, p. 27.
8. Sylvia Nasar, "The American Economy, Back on Top," *The New York Times*, February 27, 1994, section 3, p.7.
9. Nasar, p. 7.
10. Charles Clotfelter, Ronald Ehrenburg, Malcolm Getz, and John Siegfried, *Economic Challenges in Higher Education* (Chicago: University of Chicago Press, 1991).
11. Ibid.
12. National Center for Education Statistics, *Digest of Education Statistics 1992* (Washington, DC: U.S. Department of Education, 1992), p. 34.
13. D. Kent Halstead, *Higher Education Revenues and Expenditures: A Study of Institutional Costs* (Washington, DC: Research Associates of Washington, 1991), pp. 194–196; D. Kent Halstead, *Inflation Measures for Schools and Colleges: 1993 Update* (Washington, DC: Research Associates of Washington, 1993).
14. Howard R. Bowen, "The Art of Retrenchment," in *Academe 69, no. 1* (January–February 1983): 21.
15. Howard Bowen, *The Costs of Higher Education: How Much Do Colleges and Universities Spend per Student and How Much Should They Spend?* (San Francisco: Jossey-Bass Inc., 1980), pp. 30–31.
16. Editors of *The Chronicle of Higher Education, The Almanac of Higher Education 1994* (Chicago: University of Chicago Press, 1994).
17. Sean C. Rush and Sandra L. Johnson, *The Decaying American Campus: A Ticking Time Bomb* (Alexandria, VA: Association of Physical Plant Administrators of Universities and Colleges, 1989), pp. 12–14.
18. Hans H. Jenny with Geoffrey C. Hughes and Richard P. Devine, *Hang-

Gliding, or Looking for an Updraft: A Study of College and University Finance in the 1980s—The Capital Margin (Wooster, OH and Boulder, CO: The College of Wooster and John Minter Associates, 1981).

19. Charles J. Anderson, Deborah J. Carter, and Andrew G. Malizio, with Boichi San, *1989–90 Fact Book on Higher Education* (New York: American Council on Education, 1989), p. 50.

20. National Center for Education Statistics, *Digest of Educational Statistics* (Washington, DC: U.S. Department of Education, 1992), p. 41.

21. Paul E. Lingenfelter and Freeman H. Beets, *Higher Education Financing Policies: States/Institutions and Their Interaction* (Kansas City, MO: U.S. Department of Education, Region VII, 1980), p. 15.

22. This section is adapted from Howard Bowen, *The Costs of Higher Education: How Much Do Colleges and Universities Spend per Student and How Much Should They Spend?* (San Francisco: Jossey-Bass Inc., 1980), pp. 76–100.

23. Lingenfelter and Beets, p. 21.

24. Gail Franck, Richard E. Anderson, and Clark Bernard, "Tax Reform and Higher Education," in Richard E. Anderson and Joel W. Meyerson, eds., *Financing Higher Education: Strategies After Tax Reform*, New Directions for Higher Education no. 58 (San Francisco: Jossey-Bass Inc., 1987), pp. 9–20.

25. Louis T. Benezet, *Private Higher Education and Public Funding*, AAHE-ERIC Higher Education Research Report no. 5 (Washington, DC: American Association for Higher Education, 1976).

26. "Revenues and Expenditures of Colleges and Universities, 1990–91," *The Chronicle of Higher Education, Almanac Issue* (August 25, 1993): 39.

27. Marilyn McCoy and D. Kent Halstead, *Higher Education Financing in the Fifty States: Interstate Comparisons, FY 1979* (Boulder, CO: National Center for Higher Education Management, 1982), p. 12.

28. Andersen, Carter, Malizio, with San.

29. Ibid.

30. Ibid., pp. 44–45.

31. Kristin Keough, *Current Funds Revenues and Expenditures of Institutions of Higher Education: Fiscal Years 1982–1990* (Washington, DC: U.S. Department of Education, National Center for Education Statistics, 1992), p. 14.

32. Ibid.

33. James J. Rusk and Larry L. Leslie, "The Setting of Tuition in Public Higher Education," in *Journal of Higher Education 49, no. 6* (November/December 1978): 531–547.

34. Charles S. Length, *The Tuition Dilemma—State Policies and Practices in Pricing Public Higher Education* (Denver: State Higher Education Executive Officers, 1993), p. 7.

35. *The Chronicle of Higher Education, Almanac Issue* (September 6, 1989): 15.

36. Keough, p. 14.

37. Benezet, p. 27.

38. Keough.

39. Ibid.

40. Ibid.
41. National Association of College and University Business Officers, *NACUBO Endowment Study* (Washington: NACUBO, 1994).

42. Editors of *The Chronicle of Higher Education, The Almanac of Higher Education* (Chicago: University of Chicago Press, 1994), p. 76.
43. Ibid.
44. Association of Governing Boards of Universities and Colleges and the National Association of College and University Business Officers, *Financial Responsibilities of Governing Boards of Colleges and Universities* (Washington: AGB and NACUBO, 1979), p. 29.
45. *The Almanac of Higher Education*, p. 76.
46. Ibid.

THREE
The Budget Process

Budgeting in higher education has so many universal characteristics that the process can be generalized to both the public and
the independent sectors. In the macroperspective, the actors in
the process, the roles they play, the timing of their participation, and the
sequence of events in the budget cycle are remarkably similar from one
institution to another. The roles performed by the actors provide a
framework for budgetary behavior. One person or office may assume
different roles depending on the stage of the process.

Differences reflect distinctions in institutional character: institutional size; administrative sophistication; faculty governance structures
and processes; the degree of centralization of decision-making authority;
the amount of trust among administrators, faculty, and students; the
openness of the budgetary process; and the demand for information.

Budget cycles overlap, thereby increasing the complexity of the process. At any one time, budgeters are involved in multiple cycles that de-
rive from preceding cycles. In this sense, the most important
determinant of the current budget is the previous year's budget.
Budgeters generally adopt incremental decision-making strategies in
which the shape of previous budgets is retained, with the changes affecting only a small fraction of the total budget. To add to the complexity,
the operating and capital budget cycles frequently encompass different
timetables in the same fiscal year.

49

Roles

Aaron Wildavsky defines roles as "the expectations of behavior attached to institutional positions."[1] The concept of roles is a simple tool for understanding human interaction. All groups—families, classes, athletic teams, and office staffs—interact according to repertoires of behavior that are reasonably predictable depending on the particular circumstance. In the budget process, roles involve characteristic behaviors in situations that tend to recur year in and year out. Wildavsky also observes that "the roles fit in with one another and set up a stable pattern of mutual expectations, which do a great deal to reduce the burden of calculations for the participants."[2] In other words, based on the expected behavior of other actors, participants can begin to estimate the consequences of their actions. In the budget process, actors can assume multiple roles at different stages in the budget cycle.

Although models of role behavior identify a spectrum of distinct roles, the simplest budgeting model contains the "spender" or advocate role and the "cutter" or restraining role. As an advocate, for example, the department chairperson's goal is at minimum to maintain the department's current resource base, and at best to acquire as many additional resources as possible. Requesting fewer resources than currently available is usually viewed negatively by clientele groups (departmental faculty) because such behavior does not satisfy the role of advocate. An increased budget is symbolic evidence of success and represents an expansion of services; an added subspecialty in the discipline; additional enrollments; improved personnel benefits, such as satisfactory pay raises for the faculty; or a combination of these.

If the role of the department chairperson is that of advocate for additional resources, what is the role of the dean responsible for several departments? On the one hand, to the chief academic officer the dean is an advocate for all of the departments and will strive to gain as many new resources as possible. The dean's mission is not simply one of resource maximization, however, because there may be programs within the college that the dean believes should not grow or should be reduced in scope. From the point of view of the total college budget, however, the dean will not wish to lose resources. On the other hand, the dean probably could not justify a budget request that is simply the cumulative total of each department's request. The dean must exercise some discretion in assembling the request, resulting in certain departmental requests being reduced in accordance with priorities. Thus, the dean assumes the role of cutter in restraining departmental growth. His or her success in the budget process is measured in terms of the ability to gain additional resources for the college and to restrain departmental desires so as to arrive at an overall reasonable budget request.

Within a campus the budget office is often viewed as a cutter whose role is to ensure fiscal responsibility and the prudent management of resources. As seen by state agencies, however, the campus budget office is an advocate for an increased institutional budget. In the public sector this spender-cutter duality also appears in the higher levels of the budget process, extending to the governor and the governor's budget office and to the legislature and legislative fiscal staffs.

The spender-cutter model summarizes a set of expectations. Advocates often ask for more resources than they really need because they know that the cutters will reduce budgets regardless of the amounts requested. The cutters will reduce budget requests, knowing that the requests are padded and that by cutting the budgets there is little danger of injuring programs. This behavior demonstrates the built-in pressure for expansion that characterizes most budget processes.

Factors that Shape the Budget Process

Figure 3.1 outlines the most important factors that shape the budget at any college or university.

Figure 3.1 Factors that Shape the Budget Process

- ☐ Institutional character
- ☐ The participants and the roles they assume
- ☐ Openness of participation and communication
- ☐ Centralization of decision-making authority
- ☐ Demand for information

Institutional Character

The character of an institution shapes the budgeting process. Character is composed of factors such as history, mission, array of academic programs, size, geographic location, public or independent charter, profile of faculty and staff, quality of leadership, financial condition, composition of the student body, degree of faculty participation in governance, alumni support, and reputation of athletic teams. Character tends to change slowly over time.

Character determines the uniqueness of an institution; for example, the character of a state land-grant research university is different from that of a state college or state regional university or a community college. An urban public institution satisfies the needs of a different clientele than a rural institution. The geographic location, percentage of commuter students, attractiveness to various constituencies, array of degree programs, degree-granting authority, degree of political support in the legislature, and history all contribute to the character of the institution. The same differences characterize independent institutions. Thus, Harvard University, the University of Chicago, and Stanford University are distinguished independent institutions, but each has a very different character than the others.

Each dimension of an institution's character contributes to the way in which participants in the budgetary process interact. Smaller colleges and universities or large campuses located in small, close-knit communities are more conducive to shared governance and broader faculty and student participation in the budget process. In large institutions, with many departments and interest groups, faculty may be more reluctant to delegate authority to a small group of colleagues. Because it is more difficult to maintain adequate communication among faculty and administrators in large institutions, these institutions may also require more attention and resources to governance processes and communication.

Participants in the budget process at public colleges and universities and at well-endowed and prestigious independent institutions that have relatively steady sources of revenue will establish different parameters for the budget process and ask different questions about the internal allocation of resources than budgeters in institutions that are financially insecure. Public institutions are accountable to a broader constituency, including legislators and the general public, than are independent colleges and universities. Typically, public institutions must respond to more requests for information from external agencies. These demands for information shape the formats for budget requests, accounting structures, and the methodology for financial audits. Similarly, institutions (both public and independent) whose students are heavily dependent on federal or state aid must use considerable resources to account for these funds.

As a management technique, budgeting is approached in many different ways. It is not unusual for budgeters to look at how other organizations budget, with an eye to refining their own methodologies. Organizational theorists note that more change within organizations occurs by copying other organizations than from innovation. In higher education, it is often easier and cheaper to adapt proven models from other settings rather than to create instructional programs, instructional methodologies, administrative structures, and computing systems. For example, responsibility center budgeting (discussed in chapter 4) has been implemented at a handful of institutions that are now viewed as test beds for an innovative budget technique.

Grafting the new to the existing is most successful when done with a sensitivity to institutional character. For example, academic programs in the Northeast designed to attract African-American students will probably be more successful in urban institutions than in rural ones. Similarly, an institution's character and the nature of its decision-making process will determine how successfully certain budget methodologies can be adopted.

The nature of campus decision making has implications for the budget process. A large university that has a history of strong administrative guidance and limited faculty involvement may not welcome a collegial, participatory form of decision making. A large, urban state university can make little use of the budget decision-making mechanisms of Princeton University, which has a small, tightly knit intellectual and social community. Other dimensions of institutional character also affect the way budget innovations can be transported from one setting to another.

Participation

The role of administrators, faculty, and students in the decision-making process in colleges and universities and the quantity and quality of that participation are ongoing governance issues that color the budget process at individual institutions. As active participants in the design and implementation of instructional, research, and service programs, faculty often demand a role in allocating resources among programs and activities. As consumers of educational programs, students are concerned about the financial support of their programs. Although students generally are less active in campus governance than faculty or administrators, students have a major impact on the flow of resources to instructional programs through enrollment patterns. In other words, students vote on the distribution of instructional resources by choosing to enroll in certain programs.

The elements of who participates in the formal budget planning process and when they do so generally change at most colleges and universities over time. Administrators, faculty, and students seeking a broader role in the allocation of resources do not always have realistic expectations of what that participation means. Generally, participation in the budget process is not democratic. Most budget cycles have tight schedules that discourage wide involvement and leisurely consideration of major issues. The pressure of limited time is compounded when participants must deal with budget reductions. Making budget decisions concerning educational and support programs requires considerable knowledge of the relationships among campus activities. Because this knowledge and expertise is acquired gradually, a rapid turnover of participants results in discontinuities in the budget process. Also, active participation in the budget process requires a very large commitment of time, even when participants are not involved in day-to-day budgeting.

Different governance structures require different levels of participation. Moreover, participants can enter the formal budget planning process at a number of different stages. At Princeton University, for example, the governance structure encourages a high degree of participation by faculty, staff, and students. The budget process is woven tightly into the governance processes of the university community at all stages. A more common model for faculty participation in budgeting is the advisory committee. A committee actively involved in the budget process will establish the framework for analysis by addressing questions of policy issues, funding priorities, alternative income and expenditure projections, budget format, and timing. Active committees are evidenced by substantial consensus building. Less active faculty advisory committees are often asked to consider a narrower range of issues, or issues that are of secondary importance.

Some colleges and universities structure formal participation in the budget process to occur at key points during the budget cycle. Faculty, student, and administrative budget committees may be only peripherally involved in major budget decision making. The most practical role for faculty and students is to help establish program and activity priorities and recommend general levels of expenditure. Faculty participation is appropriate and useful in evaluating proposals from deans or program heads for the allocation of faculty positions. A disappointing reality of active participation is that students are pulled away from their studies and faculty are drawn away from teaching and research more than they expect.

Budgetary planning differs from day-to-day budgeting. Formal budget planning deals with campus priorities and directions and the related broad-brush distribution of resources. Within that context, budgeters, usually administrators, implement the budget on a daily basis. These day-to-day actions can cumulatively involve significant amounts and can shift campus priorities; budgeters must be able to make fiscal adjustments to meet changing considerations. For example, tuition revenue may be higher or lower than projected if enrollments are higher or lower than expected; changes in interest rates affect the expected return on investments; the roof may blow off the administrative building and need immediate replacement. How professional budgeters are held accountable to the directions set by the formal budget process differs widely from campus to campus.

Administrators are usually given the responsibility for implementing the decisions and maneuvering the process on a day-to-day basis. Practically, faculty and student participants can be involved in budget planning but not in the day-to-day administration of budgets.

Trust. The smoothness with which the budget cycle progresses is determined in large part by the degree of trust among participants at all levels. Relationships among public institutions and state agencies are just as important as those within institutions. The federal government's attitude in the early 1990s toward the indirect costs of research at Stanford University and other major research universities changed significantly after the Department of the Navy discovered significant charges that should never have been recorded. Any trust that had existed between the federal government and research universities was severely diminished, and major research universities suffered the consequences of the lack of trust by disallowance for some indirect costs, close scrutiny by auditors, and negative publicity.

Trust evolves over time as participants become more familiar with the expectations, value systems, and behavior of other participants. Trusting relationships tend to engender more communication and cooperation in the exchange of data, information, and analyses. Trust provides a framework for the effective and efficient engagement of the participants in the budget process.

Openness of the Process

The degree to which the budget process is open to casual review by those not actively involved in deliberations dictates the amount of flexibility decision makers have in their negotiations over the allocation of resources. The openness of the process, in turn, is determined by the institution's character and participatory structure for decision making— the greater the number of participants in the budget process, the more open the process is. At some institutions the degree of openness is carefully controlled to prevent unintended actions that might otherwise flow from budget decisions. For example, when identifying the strong and weak departments in an institution, most budgeters are cautious in making their determinations known to the larger academic community lest they create a self-fulfilling prophecy, whereby units labeled as weak in fact become weak as faculty morale deteriorates and mobile faculty members depart.

In recent years a trend has developed toward more open or public deliberations in the policy-making and decision-making arenas. This has been most pronounced in the public sector, where "sunshine" legislation mandates that most meetings of public officials be open to the public. While the more open decision-making process may permit more participants to become involved, it has the negative effect of discouraging negotiation. In the budget process, where by definition insufficient resources exist to meet all needs, bargaining is essential and usually involves making trade-offs. Most budget decision makers are reluctant to negotiate in public because they do not want to publicize the issues or items on which they have to compromise. Participants in the budget process thus prefer to negotiate privately to maintain "face" in front of their constituents.

In acknowledging that there are needs both for privacy and for increased participation and open communication, some institutions have designed the budget process to allow the interests of relevant groups to be represented while sensitive discussions about competing programs and activities are conducted. Accordingly, communications to the broader academic community are structured to minimize the negative impact that budget decisions may have on individuals, programs, and activities. In these circumstances, the need for openness in the budget process is balanced by the need for privacy during the more delicate deliberations.

Centralization of Decision-Making Authority

A continual source of tension between decision makers in any organizational setting, but especially when dealing with the allocation of resources, is determining the level of authority at which decisions should be made. A frequent complaint of decision makers at any level is that the range of issues over which they have final responsibility is limited by higher levels of authority. Senior campus officials at public institutions, for example, may complain that because the state legislature appropriates funds on a line-item basis rather than on a lump-sum basis, the legislature reduces their flexibility to allocate funds as they deem appropriate. Similarly, department chairpersons sometimes maintain that their decision-making authority is constrained by deans or vice chancellors who establish ceilings for departmental budget requests or who must approve departmental expenditures above a certain dollar threshold. Final decisions on tenure, which have considerable long-term financial implications, were once decided within the college but are now often made at the campus or system level.

At what level should fiscal decisions be made? Most experienced administrators would argue that final authority should be placed in the hands of those closest to the "action." However, the answer boils down to the relationship between control and accountability. Control and accountability are frequently, and quite erroneously, thought of as synonyms. In an ideal world, we would have accountability for decisions without control systems. However, some controls, be they accounting reviews or higher-level approvals for certain expenditures, are necessary for accountability. It is undesirable to control expenditures by maintaining decision-making authority at too high a level.

Decisions about the allocation of scarce resources tend to be made at higher and higher levels of authority. Especially noteworthy is the increasing professionalization of staffs at colleges and universities and the expansion of governors' budget offices and legislative fiscal staffs. Thus, the context for making decisions about resources has changed significantly. Decisions that were once made in a very informal way now evolve in a more structured manner. Accompanying the centralization of budget decision authority is the increased concern for accountability and productivity at lower levels. In such a climate it is not unusual for more documentation to be required to justify to higher authorities that resources are allocated effectively and efficiently. A major role of leaders is to provide appropriate decision-making authority and sufficient flexibility at all levels of the process.

Demand for Information

The budget cycle is structured to transmit information concerning program activities, the utilization of resources, the anticipated resource requirements of programs, or criteria for performance evaluation. When changes in the budget process are introduced (e.g., new formats for the presentation of budget materials or new budget techniques), the process will not be smooth until the participants become familiar with the changes. Disturbances arise in that familiar information is missing and the relevance of information is not clearly understood. This can be costly in terms of time and emotional involvement because participants must adjust their expectations about the kinds of information transmitted and the kinds of analyses and decisions that they must contribute to the process. A reasonably stable process enables participants to anticipate their responsibilities and reduces some of the uncertainty of budgeting. This is not to argue against change; it is to suggest that changes should be justified with respect to the costs incurred.

As the number of staff at all levels increases and as decisions about the allocation of resources move to higher levels of authority, the demand for information increases. In California, for example, during the growth years of the 1960s and 1970s, officials at the University of California used an informal index whereby three additional university staff members were needed to handle the increased demand for information for each additional staff person hired at the state level. Greater involvement by professional staff in academic decision making also often leads to more sophisticated analyses, which in turn require more information. This causal relationship also entails a more sophisticated framework for budgeting. The preparation of more sophisticated analyses is an appropriate goal; the hiring of staff members who only make work for other staff members is not.

Decision makers are often frustrated by the fact that information tends to flow upward in the authority hierarchy. In comparison to the amount of information provided to higher-level decision makers, the amount flowing downward as feedback generally seems small. Decision makers sometimes argue that the information imbalance exists because their responsibilities do not allow sufficient time to formulate appropriate messages to subordinate levels. There are, however, two additional explanations. First, decision makers tend to collect more information than they can use; and second, they underestimate the information needs of those lower in the hierarchy and do not structure effective feedback channels. The two-way flow of information in the budget process is especially important as participants negotiate for resources and adjust their positions to reflect changes in the demands of other participants, the priorities of senior decision makers, and the availability of resources.

Operating Budget/Capital Budget Duality

In any fiscal year, two distinct but interconnected budgets exist simultaneously: the operating budget, which addresses all activities related to campus operations, and the capital budget, which addresses physical changes and additions to the buildings and grounds of the campus.

Operating and capital budgets often have programmatic overlap. Deferred maintenance, which includes repairs to the physical environment that do not alter the size or function of the facility (e.g., replacing entire roofs or windows), typically is funded from the operating budget. Modest physical changes, such as relocating an office wall or a door, are also typically funded from the operating budget. (Most institutions have a dollar threshold above which projects are capitalized and funded from the capital budget.) New facilities, significant renovations of existing facilities, and campus infrastructure (e.g., power plants, utility conduits, roads) are funded by the capital budget. Capital projects influence the operating budget in that the costs, either increased or decreased, to clean, light, heat, and cool the new or renovated space must be recognized.

Operating and capital budgets have different time horizons, which influence how they are prepared, implemented, and funded. The operating budget usually covers the expenditures for campus operations for one year in settings with an annual budget or two years in settings with a biennial budget. This is not to say that operating budget expenditures are not proposed within a multiyear framework. Many, in fact, are. The operating budget highlights the proposed expenditures for the next budget cycle only. Major capital projects can extend over four or five years: program planning, the preparation of schematic drawings, and the preparation of construction drawings can each consume a year, while the actual construction can take two years or more for large projects. Accordingly, funding is phased for capital projects to reflect the expected duration of each step.

In public higher education the two budgets are prepared and reviewed separately, sometimes because the source of revenues for each may differ. In California, for example, voters are asked to approve separate initiatives for capital programs in different sectors of the public arena (e.g., higher education, prisons). Generally, capital and operating budgets have different processes for preparation and review, although the timetables may be such that the deadlines for submission of operating and capital budget requests, and the time allowed for their review, may be the same. In the independent sector the operating and capital budgets tend to be more closely linked because both are generally funded from the same sources; in some institutions the capital and operating budgets are combined.

In both the public and the independent sectors, the method used to finance capital projects funded from nonstate or private money can influence the operating budget. If all the funding needed for an entire capital project is available now, through a bequest, grant, savings, or a combination thereof, the operating budget is not affected (except for changes in utilities expenses and the operation and maintenance of the physical plant). If, however, the capital project is financed through a loan, the annual debt service must be included in the operating budget. A converse situation can occur when a major facility is leased, and the lease costs are included in the operating budget. In some circumstances the lease is considered as capitalized, which means that the value of the facility is included in calculations of debt capacity for the institution.

Implications of the Capital Budget for the Operating Budget

Many institutions neglect to consider the relationship of the capital budget to the annual operating budget. This lack of coordination is particularly striking in public institutions, where the capital and annual operating budgets are often treated as distinct entities.

The capital budget typically addresses new equipment needs, replacement of obsolete or worn-out equipment, renovation of existing facilities, and acquisition of new facilities. In the best of circumstances, the capital budget is prepared on the basis of a long-range plan for the capital needs of academic programs and support units.

There is no uniformity in higher education in the accounting standards for capital depreciation. In fact, a lively debate continues over whether capital depreciation is a realistic concept for colleges and universities. Opponents contend that facilities and equipment wear out and should not be depreciated. Capital depreciation, they argue, is valid only in the for-profit sector in relation to taxes. From this perspective, financial support for the replacement of facilities and equipment should come from gifts and endowment income restricted to that purpose. (In fact, capital projects can also be funded through debt financing.) Capital depreciation is an especially sensitive subject in the public sector, where government agencies seem to want to keep capital outlays out of the spotlight. Generally, public institutions do not depreciate their capital facilities. Instead, they request replacements through the capital budget process.

A more practical and realistic approach to capital budgeting, especially in the independent sector, is to build a depreciation charge into the annual operating budget. This charge would be over and above the portion of the annual operating budget devoted to preventive maintenance. The size of the annual capital charge would be set on the basis of a long-range plan for capital development. The money would be placed in a reserve fund as a means for removing it from the cash flow for use in present and future capital projects. Charging the annual operating budget for depreciation seems to offer more certainty in the capital budgeting process than depending on the timely beneficence of donors.

Participants in the budget process will probably find that capital needs are often seen as less urgent than annual operating needs. Thus, the capital component of the annual operating budget may be seen as a primary candidate for reductions to balance the institution's budget. This tendency to see the capital budget as a source of painless cuts should be avoided. Reducing or eliminating a capital depreciation charge from the annual operating budget is trading a short-term financial difficulty for a long-term one that will likely be more debilitating. For example, Yale University suddenly realized in the late 1980s that its physical plant had deteriorated to such an extent that it was required to invest tens of millions of dollars in short order to keep its facilities functioning. A more systematic program of deferred maintenance and capital depreciation probably would have avoided the fiscal shock that Yale University experienced.

The Budget Cycle

Overlapping Cycles

The temporal overlap in budget cycles strongly influences the behavior of participants. In both the independent and the public sectors, more than one budget cycle is considered at the same time. Figure 3.2 illustrates the annual operating budget cycle for Stanford University; figure 3.3 illustrates the budget cycle for the University of Maryland, College Park. The fiscal year at Stanford extends from September 1 through August 31. In figure 3.2, while the FY 1987–88 budget was being executed, the FY 1988–89 budget was being prepared. Research, analyses, and forecasting for the FY 1988–89 budget were performed prior to the beginning of FY 1987–88. Budget instructions for FY 1988–89 were prepared and distributed just as FY 1987–88 began. Thus, participants in the budget process drew on their experience during FY 1986–87 to plan for the FY 1988–89 budget. In a sense, the most important determinant of

Figure 3.2 The Annual Operating Budget Cycle
Stanford University

September/October	Budget staff and local units review prior year's planning and budgeting results.
October	Provost sets three-year planning parameters for local units.
November/December	Local units prepare and submit three-year operating and financial plans in constant dollars.
December	Long-range financial forecast is discussed with trustees and faculty senate.
January	Provost adjusts planning parameters based on review of three-year plans and university priorities.
January/February	Local units plan and propose following year's budget in nominal dollars using revised planning parameters and cost-rise factors.
March	Provost sets size of nominal budget for each unit ("block budget").
	Tuition, room, and board proposals go to the board of trustees.
April/May	Local units optimize within block, prepare detail of budget, propose salaries.
	Operating budget guidelines are reported to the senate and recommended to the board of trustees.
June	Service center and auxiliary budgets are reviewed.
July/August	Salaries are announced.
August	Final budget is published.

Source: *Stanford University Operating Budget Guidelines*, 1988–89

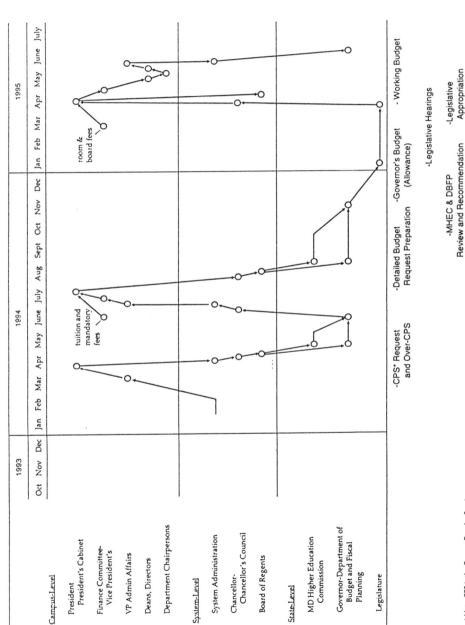

Figure 3.3 Fiscal 1995 Operating Budget Development Process — University of Maryland, College Park

* Note: CPS is the Current Peoples Service

the FY 1988–89 budget was the 1987–88 budget, which was beginning to be played out as the 1988–89 budget was being assembled.

The University of Maryland, College Park, has a longer schedule for budget preparation because of the involvement of state-level agencies. The fiscal year at Maryland extends from July 1 through June 30. Campus officials were required to prepare a preliminary estimate of their budget needs for FY 1995–96 more than 16 months before the fiscal year was to begin. Based on the campus estimate of needs and state-level projections of revenue availability, the governor set a ceiling in June 1994 for FY 1995–96. The guidelines for the campus budget for FY 1995–96 were established, therefore, during FY 1993–94.

The budget cycle for public institutions is even longer in states with biennial budgets. Institutional estimates of budget needs for the second year of the biennium are based on the budget from three years before. Much can happen in the two to three years between budget estimation and the beginning of the fiscal year that can make the budget obsolete, particularly during times of rapid economic change. State legislatures are becoming increasingly aware of this problem and are scheduling more interim sessions to discuss and amend the state's budget for the second year of a biennium. In any case, budgeters cannot effect change in the overall shape of the budget for at least two years because prior budgets are already largely established.

When projecting so far into the future, budgeters reduce their uncertainty by using current experience as a base. Adjustments are made at the margin to reflect anticipated changes in revenues and expenditures, which in turn are determined by a host of variables, including program mix, enrollments, the market for new faculty, inflation factors, and investment yields. Scheduled changes such as the introduction of a new degree program or tighter admissions standards can be planned for, but it is difficult to predict more radical disturbances such as new environmental regulations, skyrocketing interest rates, reductions in federal student assistance, and the impact of national economic trends on the institution's enrollment base. Accordingly, budgeters build budgets on the historical base adjusted incrementally.

Except for the schedule of events, the budget cycle is similar for both public and independent institutions, although it is longer in the public sector because of the involvement of state-level agencies. The budget cycles described below are generalized for both sectors. The cycles of specific institutions may vary in terms of sequence and actors. In the following discussion, the chronology of events assumes a fiscal year beginning July 1.

Independent Colleges and Universities

A number of large independent institutions have adopted a responsibility-centered (or profit-centered) approach to budgeting during the past decade (see Appendix). In this model, individual schools and colleges within the university are given control of their own revenues (i.e., tuition and fees, research funds, overhead money from research funding, income from endowments credited to the school or college, gifts earmarked for the school or college) and responsibility for managing their own budgets. The central administration, including support services, is supported by a tax on school and college income. Schools that have insufficient revenue of their own may be subsidized through the same kind of tax. For example, schools or colleges of letters and science typically have a more difficult time than specific professional schools in generating sufficient revenue to be self-supporting, and need to be subsidized through a revenue-sharing arrangement. The taxation scheme needs to be founded on solid academic values that are widely shared by the campus community.

The description that follows of the budget cycle in independent institutions is applicable to settings with responsibility-centered budgeting. (Figure 3.4 provides an example of the budgeting cycle at such an institution.) Schools and colleges are held accountable for their income, but have more autonomy in managing their budgets. The central administration must allocate money to support activities and schools and colleges with insufficient income.

Analyses and projections. Participants in the budget process, including presidents, deans, department chairpersons, faculty, directors of administrative support units, and students, need to be given a framework within which they can present their justifications for resource requests. Unless participants are all working under the same assumptions and constraints, budget requests will not be congruent and information from lower levels, such as departments and administrative support units, will have to be ignored or collected anew at higher levels.

Figure 3.4 The Budget Cycle at an Independent Institution, July 1, 1995–June 30, 1996

April 1994–August 1994	Analyses and projections are performed by the chief fiscal officer, the controller's office, the budget office, and the office of institutional studies.
August 1994	Budget preparation instructions are issued by the institution's central budget officers, including the chief fiscal officer, the director of the budget, and the chief academic officer or dean of the faculty.
August 1994–September 1994	Units prepare their requests.
September 1994	Departmental budget requests are submitted.
September 1994–October 1994	Departmental budget requests are reviewed and consolidated at the college level.
October 1994–January 1995	College-level requests are reviewed by the institutional president, the chief financial or business officer, the chief academic officer, the budget office, and staff members concerned directly with budgeting.
January 1995–March 1995	The president provides formal budget recommendations to the governing board's finance committee.
February 1995–March 1995	Governing board approves budget recommendations.
February 1995–May 1995	Subsequent to board's approval of the budget, staff prepare detailed budgets reflecting changes in revenues or in programs or activities.
July 1, 1995	Fiscal year 1996 begins.

This framework for budgeting, often called budget instructions, budget protocol, or budget guidelines, must in turn be informed by analyses and projections of conditions in years to come. These projections and analyses are normally carried out during spring or summer, some 15 to 10 months prior to the beginning of the fiscal year. Analyses include:

- estimates of the impact on enrollment of changes in admissions standards, changes in program offerings, and changes in federal student assistance programs and the availability of aid funds;
- estimates of income for several years, including investment income, gifts, tuition, and research funding;
- estimates of expenses for several years, including anticipated increases in faculty and staff salaries, the impact of changing energy costs and regulatory requirements, the cost of periodicals, the cost of bringing new or renovated facilities into operation, and the impact of the CPI on the cost of goods and services;
- estimates of the impact of affirmative action programs; and
- a proposed plan of action to reconcile the budget experience of recent years with the anticipated conditions of the next several years.

A number of institutions involve faculty in reviewing the overall constraints set and the particular budget framework used.

The degree of sophistication of the projections and analyses depends largely on the staff resources available, the experience of the analysts, and the accuracy and availability of information (larger institutions tend to have more staff resources and more highly developed information systems than smaller institutions). Participants in the preliminary analytical tasks often include the chief fiscal officer, the controller's office, the budget office, the office of institutional studies, and the office of institutional planning. The chief academic officer may be involved in assessing the effects of changes in the instructional programs. In smaller institutions, the projections may be done by a handful of individuals, such as the chief fiscal or business officer, the director of the budget, and the chief academic officer. In both large and small institutions, considerable time and effort is devoted to updating and correcting information. At the preliminary analysis stage, most formal committees are composed of administrators rather than faculty, students, or trustees.

Budget preparation instructions. Budget preparation instructions are usually issued in the early fall (ten to nine months before the fiscal year begins) by the institution's central budget officers, including the chief fiscal officer, the director of the budget, and the chief academic officer or dean of the faculty. Units have approximately one month to prepare their requests. The information contained in the instructions and the manner in which it is presented vary depending on the intended purpose. At some institutions, for example, the budget instructions or guidelines are distributed to as much of the campus community as possible. In such instances the instructions are designed to present an overview of the budget process, including a chronology of steps, the institution's long-range context and outlook, a discussion of particular budget problems for the coming year, a discussion of the assumptions for the preparation of budget requests, and tentative proposed operating budgets for the year ahead. These instructions thus become a status report that communicates proposed changes in the institution's mission and scope of operations.

Often, however, the guidelines are more technical, having been designed for individuals with responsibility for specific parts of the budget. The instructions specify the constraints under which budget requests should be prepared: estimates of inflation factors for operating expense budgets, estimates of increases in salaries and wages, and conditions under which additional faculty and staff positions can be requested.

Perhaps the most complex aspect of the budget request is the budgeting and planning for faculty positions. The complexity arises from the special nature of faculty appointments (i.e., 9, 10, 11, or 12 months), the vastly different market conditions for faculty members in different disciplines, the flexible schedules and assignments of faculty, and the looseness of departmental organization. Budget instructions must address such issues as:

□ enrollment trends and their implications for staffing;
□ the distribution of tenured and nontenured permanent faculty;
□ the distribution of part-time faculty;
□ anticipated tenure and promotion decisions;
□ anticipated sponsored research and its effect on faculty salary needs;
□ anticipated faculty leaves of absence without pay and sabbatical leaves;

☐   the effect of gifts and endowments restricted to the particular department;
☐   the distribution of teaching loads among the faculty; and
☐   the instructional workload of the department as a whole.

Faculty salaries and benefits make up the largest single part of the budget; therefore, plans for faculty staffing greatly influence the budget. Also, because most colleges and universities employ permanent faculty on the basis of contracts of three or more years and tenure commitments, the financial impact of staffing decisions will be felt for many years.

Many institutions with faculties that are stable or shrinking in size are concerned about the prospect of departments with a very high percentage of tenured faculty and therefore little flexibility to hire young faculty members. To assure the inflow of new faculty, some institutions have developed quota systems that limit the percentage of tenured faculty by department or college or by entire campus. Other institutions, more consistent with policy espoused by the American Association of University Professors, have avoided such quotas. Where long-term staffing plans exist, the annual budget instructions often specify for each department or college the number of tenured positions available, the number of new positions that can be filled, and the number of positions that must be relinquished for purposes of reallocation.

Estimates of operating expenses and support staff costs for academic and nonacademic units are much more straightforward and are usually based on the application of inflation factors for the costs of goods and services to the operating expenses base, to workload data, and to tentative salary adjustments for administrators and support staff. Requests for additional staff must usually be justified in detail with respect to changes in organization, service loads, and unit mission.

Designers of budget instructions often give too little consideration to the information burdens placed on department chairpersons, deans, and the heads of administrative units. Much of what is demanded is a verification of the existing situation; data are used by participants at higher levels to correct and update their databases. In an attempt to reduce some of the paperwork and effort and to introduce simpler requests for information, some colleges and universities have eliminated the more routine budget forms, requesting information for exceptions only. Thus, departments or administrative units must respond only when modifications in the level of operations or changes in the source of funding are proposed.

The departmental budget request. Departmental structure, plan of organization, and bylaws determine the level of faculty and student participation in assembling the departmental budget request. In any case, the department chairperson assumes a major responsibility for justifying the department's resource needs to higher levels.

There is considerable variation from one institution to another and from one department to another in terms of the internal guidelines used to prepare requests. In some cases the department has a formal long-term plan for developing its instructional, research, and service programs. In other cases, either the chairperson has a plan of action in mind or an implicit understanding exists among the faculty about how the department is to develop. This plan is usually related to the services to be rendered, including the number of sections to be taught, class size, committee assignments, and time for research. Generally, departments that have weak leadership do not have a strong basis for preparing and justifying requests and seek to maintain the status quo in their budgets.

Larger institutions tend to consolidate departmental budget requests by college or school. Again the college structure, plan of organization, and bylaws will determine the level of participation in preparing the request. Department chairpersons are largely responsible for defending their unit's needs during the process. For those cases where the college budget is not simply the sum of departmental requests, the college dean may act as the first level of formal review in the budget process and may hold budget hearings and perform analyses.

Ideally, departments will prepare a consolidated budget, including salaries, wages, and operating expenses. Then departments can present a complete picture of their resource needs to higher levels. However, some colleges and universities have separate budget requests for faculty and administrative support staffing and operating expenses, or allow academic departments to request additional staff throughout the year. The piecemeal nature of these requests gives the departments some flexibility to make last-minute changes because of factors such as faculty resignations or the availability of a leading scholar, though this makes the preparation of budget requests a continual process at the departmental level. Requests that change during the budget cycle place additional administrative burdens on the department and make it difficult for campus-level officials to review competing program and activity needs simultaneously.

Review of budget requests. Budget requests are normally reviewed and analyzed each time they are consolidated for presentation to a higher level of the process, until an institutional budget is ultimately presented to the governing board for consideration. Informal reviews occur during preparation of budget requests as department chairpersons discuss the budget situation with their deans, and administrative unit heads with their superiors. The purpose of these discussions is twofold: to encourage the requesting units to be realistic in stating their resource needs, and to provide the first level of reviewers with information about resource needs so that they can begin their analyses.

College-level review. In large institutions with multiple colleges and schools, the first level of review is usually at the college level and is held nine to eight months before the fiscal year begins. Typically, the dean consolidates individual departmental requests into a single college request; unless the departments have exercised considerable restraint, the dean will have to pare the requests to generate a college request that will appear reasonable to campus-level reviewers. Many colleges do not have the luxury of a large administrative staff, so analysis of departmental requests tends to be limited. The dean may assemble a faculty advisory committee to make recommendations or may prepare the college request without formal participation of faculty. In either case departmental chairpersons may be consulted frequently. Where a formal plan for academic programs does not exist, the college request is shaped by recommendations from advisory committees or the dean's staff. Questions raised at the dean's level focus largely on academic issues: curriculum design, course scheduling, faculty staffing, program enrollments, and research agendas. There is usually considerable informal interaction between the college and campus levels during college-level reviews, particularly when resources are limited. For example, college-level officials may request updates of revenue projections, assistance in performing analyses, or information concerning the use of endowment income and restricted funds.

Campus-level review. The major review of departmental and college budget requests and requests from administrative units occurs about nine to five months before the fiscal year begins. The major participants in the campus-level review are the president, the chief financial or business officer, the chief academic officer, the budget office, and staff members concerned directly with budgeting. Participation in the process beyond this circle varies from campus to campus. Hearings where academic and administrative officials can defend their budget requests are held as is necessary or customary. Many institutions have advisory committees that make recommendations to the president. Princeton University, for example, has a Priorities Committee that, by acting as an advisor to the president, performs thorough analyses and makes specific, detailed recommendations. This committee is composed of faculty, graduate and undergraduate students, and members of the administration and staff. At Stanford University, the University Advisory Committee on Budget Planning examines issues of long-range importance, reviews the major assumptions for each year's budget planning, and advises the president on planning problems and prospects.

In some institutions, faculty senates assign to faculty committees the responsibility for an independent review of budget requests. During the campus-level review, the governing board is often involved, normally through a finance or budget committee. This committee is kept informed about the long-range financial forecast for the institution and about the progress of staff and advisory committee reviews and analyses. The president usually provides the board's budget or finance committee with formal budget recommendations six to five months before the fiscal year begins.

Considerable attention is given to sources of funding. Budget staff regularly refine estimates of income from sources over which the institution has limited control, including endowment, gifts, and contracts and grants. Student enrollment projections are updated to reflect the institution's fall semester or quarter experience and are applied against alternative tuition and fee schedules to yield a range of income estimates. Ceilings for departmental and college budget requests in the academic area and for support activity requests are adjusted to fit available resources.

Budget staff and members of advisory committees analyze the various components of budget requests in such categories as faculty staffing, computing, library facilities, special academic programs, physical plant, academic administration, general administration, faculty and staff salary adjustments, tuition, and student aid. The student aid budget is dependent in large part on anticipated tuition levels and current federal student assistance policies. Budget requests for self-supporting activities, including faculty and staff housing, student housing, food services, intercollegiate athletics, and various services, are analyzed separately in terms of rate structures, projected revenues, and the impact of rates on other campus units. Capital construction needs are also reviewed.

In conjunction with the revenue estimation and activity analyses, key administrators negotiate among themselves and with the units under their control to reshape activity and program plans to fit resource constraints. This process of negotiation is continual, beginning at the earliest stages of the budget process, and is a response to both the changing nature of activities and programs—such as the sudden replacement of building systems, the implementation of new degree programs, the opportunity to hire an outstanding faculty member, and the upgrading of a management information system—and the changing revenue picture—including national economic trends, the number of student applications, and the receipt of a large gift from a generous alumnus.

Some institutions are more successful than others in using the budget review stage to reduce the uncertainty experienced by participants. Two problems can arise at this stage. First, the review of budget requests can be stymied if operating units and departments do not provide complete requests, or if the requests are not considered simultaneously. In situations where requests for resources cannot be examined together, budgeters must keep a tally of commitments for periodic comparison with estimates of available resources or else the various requests cannot be treated as competing claims against a fixed level of funding. Campuses that routinely permit units to request additional staffing or operating funds throughout the year and that approve these requests will be susceptible to overcommitting resources.

Second, some colleges and universities review the academic programs portion of the budget separately from the administrative support portion. This approach obscures the close relationship between academic and administrative support activities. For example, a significant increase

in a department's research activity will result in an increase in the workload of the controller's office or the sponsored programs office. Similarly, the introduction of an on-line computer requisition system can
streamline administrative activities in the purchasing department while
at the same time reduce the administrative workload in academic departments. Institutions that establish academic and administrative budgets simultaneously seem to be more successful in anticipating the fiscal
impact that activities in one area have on another.

Preparation of the detailed budget. The president makes formal budget
recommendations to the governing board six to four months before the
fiscal year begins. The board's finance or budget committee, which has
likely been involved informally in the budget review process, reports to
the full board at this time. The board of trustees acts on the general outline of the proposed budget and on specific recommendations for tuition
and fees, room and board increases, salary increases, the proportion of
endowment income to be applied to the operating budget, and student
aid. Assuming that differences of opinion have been reconciled before
the formal recommendations are presented to the board of trustees,
board approval tends to be routine. The board's interests are usually protected through the work of its budget or finance committee during the
budget process. The board evaluates the overall institutional budget
from a broad perspective, considering the institution's mission and the
implications of environmental conditions, weighing competing program
goals, and projecting the effect of current decisions on the future of the
institution.

Once the governing board approves the budget recommendations,
staff begin to prepare the detailed budget. This stage of the process generally occurs five to two months before the fiscal year begins. Adjustments are made to reflect late changes in the revenue picture or in
programs and activities.

The approval of budget recommendations and preparation of the detailed budget can be delayed at institutions that have collective bargaining agreements. The delays might occur every two or three years, the
usual frequency of negotiations for collective agreements. In the future,
unions may seek to increase the frequency of negotiations as a hedge
against the uncertainty of multiyear contracts. Because negotiations most
often take place during the spring, the amount of time available to

prepare the detailed budget will depend on how quickly an agreement can be reached. If, for example, the cost of wage increases exceeds revenue projections, the scope of operations in the academic and nonacademic areas may have to be reduced. In some situations protracted negotiations delay final settlement until well into the new fiscal year, leaving unit heads to operate for several months without firm knowledge of their new budget.

Implementation of the budget. The budget represents an expenditure plan for the institution's programs and activities. Within that plan, however, unit heads must expend their resources in accordance with the institution's accounting structure and cash-flow scheme. Accounting rules restrict the use of certain categories of funds. The cash-flow scheme regulates the expenditure of funds so that it matches as closely as possible the receipt of revenues. Departments may not be able to purchase expensive items of equipment early in the fiscal year, for example, because the institution's primary source of income—tuition and fees—is collected in the fall (for the fall semester) and spring (for the spring semester).

Expenditures are monitored closely throughout the fiscal year by the controller's office and the budget office. Staff in these offices project savings in budgeted staff salaries resulting from turnover and project fuel and utilities expenditures as well as other general operating expenditures. These same staff also regularly update income projections, flag problem areas for administrative attention, control the transfer of funds among categories to ensure compliance with accounting procedures, and compare actual enrollment patterns to the budgeted patterns to provide information for making expenditure readjustments. The controller's office usually provides periodic fund balance statements to the operating units, which can then monitor their own expenditures.

The day-to-day decisions that budgeters must make within the context of the budget framework cumulatively can involve significant resources and have wide-ranging effects on policy for subsequent fiscal years. By their very nature those operational decisions are not often scrutinized by advisory committees, and do not occur according to a fixed schedule.

Closing out the fiscal year. Most colleges and universities have procedures for the orderly closing of expenditures for the fiscal year. These procedures are intended to allow sufficient time to process paperwork and to discourage last-minute spending. For example, some institutions prohibit certain types of expenditures within 30 or 60 days of the end of the year, or change the routing of purchase requisitions to allow the budget office or the controller's office to monitor more closely the flow of funds.

All institutions perform audits to ensure that funds have been accounted for and used properly. Internal auditors work throughout the fiscal year and "perform detailed reviews of activities of the institution to apprise management of the adequacy of controls, policy compliance, procedures for safeguarding assets from fraud, and sometimes performance of employees in carrying out assigned responsibilities," according to *Financial Responsibilities of Governing Boards of Colleges and Universities,* published by NACUBO and the Association of Governing Boards of Universities and Colleges.[3] External auditors are usually private accounting firms, although state and federal auditors are considered external for institutions that receive public funds. External auditors test and evaluate the institution's internal financial controls and its compliance with financial policies, normally including in their report a management letter stating that the financial data are accurate and that the accounting systems are trustworthy. Usually, fiscal audit reports do not evaluate the programs and activities for which funds were expended, but simply account for those funds and evaluate the accounting structure. The work of external auditors complements that of internal auditors; tests performed by the external auditors are similar to those performed by the internal auditors but are not as extensive. State and federal auditors examine only specific programs and activities. Independent colleges and universities usually have up to two months to close out the previous fiscal year.

Public Colleges and Universities

The budget cycle for public institutions is similar to that for independent institutions, with two major exceptions: the cycle begins much earlier in the public sector and it includes participants at the system and state levels. Figure 3.5 provides an example of the budget cycle at a public institution.

The framework for budget requests. Most states have some form of a statewide master plan for public, and occasionally independent, postsecon-

Figure 3.5   The Budget Cycle at a Public Institution, July 1, 1995–June 30, 1996

October 1993–June 1994	Preliminary asking budget is developed by departments and reviewed at the college level; college-level budgets are then reviewed at the campus level.
	Finished preliminary budget is submitted to the governing board and forwarded, upon approval, to the appropriate state agencies.
	In institutions without formal budget cycles, institutions, state offices, and state agencies conduct informal negotiations and discussions to establish a framework.
	Budget request ceiling is established by the governor's budget office.
	Budget instructions are issued.
July 1994–October 1994	Detailed budget requests are prepared and reviewed internally.
September 1994–November 1994	Budget requests are forwarded to the governing board.
September 1994–November 1994	Institutional requests are forwarded to state agencies.
October 1994–December 1994	State executive office reviews budgets.
January 1995–April 1995	Legislature reviews budgets.
March 1995–June 1995	Appropriations are made and distributed.
July 1, 1995	Fiscal year 1996 begins.

dary education. Generally, the institutions are heavily involved in the development of such plans, primarily through advisory councils made up of faculty and administrators. The plans can specify the mission of each institution, describe the distribution of academic programs, and even establish enrollment targets. Updated regularly, these plans are an important component of the framework for budgeting in the public sector.

The structure of a state's public postsecondary education has considerable bearing on who participates in preliminary budget planning. In a multicampus university system, officials in the central administrative office may be active in establishing the budget framework for each campus, especially if the system office participates in budget negotiations with state officials. If the state higher education agency is a consolidated governing board, the central administration tends to have a dominant role in setting the framework for the campuses, whereas if the agency is a coordinating board, the degree to which the coordinating board participates in the establishment of the budget framework depends on the board's statutory authority for budget review.

To reduce the uncertainty of budgeting, some states employ a "preliminary asking budget cycle" to set institutional ceilings for the "final" asking budget requests. The preliminary asking budget cycle is a means for state-level agencies to examine institutional "blue-sky" requests, to make an early assessment of institutional needs and compare those needs with projections of the availability of state revenues, and to give institutions a realistic target for the more detailed budget requests to follow. The stages for the preliminary asking budget cycle closely parallel those of the detailed budget cycle. The difference is largely one of focus. Preparation and review of the preliminary asking budget center on the broad questions of the merits of entire programs and activities, the interrelationships of these programs and activities, and the establishment of program priorities. The preliminary asking budget cycle tends to consider major issues; the "final" asking budget cycle addresses program details. The major issues often include faculty salaries, program expansion, deferred maintenance, and research programs.

The preliminary asking budget is usually assembled and reviewed 21 to 12 months prior to the beginning of the fiscal year. Guidelines for assembling the preliminary asking budget are provided by the governor's budget office, the consolidated governing board, the multicampus system office, or a combination of these. The guidelines tend to deal with the more mechanical aspects of request submission, containing only minimal information on policies for developing budget requests. The campuses or multicampus system offices may supplement these guidelines with preliminary information to create a more issue-oriented framework for constructing requests at the department and college levels. Departmental requests are reviewed at the college level, and college-level requests are reviewed at the campus level. The range of participants, the use of hearings, and the sophistication of analyses vary widely. Because of the preliminary nature of the requests, campus-level analyses tend to be less detailed and thorough than those in settings where there is no preliminary asking budget cycle.

Campus-level recommendations are generally reviewed by the system-level administration in a multicampus structure and by the finance or budget committee of the governing board. If modifications to the campus requests are needed, the requests are returned to the campuses for adjustment. The finished preliminary request is then submitted to the governing board and, if approved, forwarded to the appropriate state agencies, which might include the higher education coordinating agency, the governor's budget office, and the legislative fiscal staff(s). The state-level review of the preliminary asking budget covers the appropriateness of new activities and programs or major expansions of existing services and the estimates of the amount of resources available for higher education. State agencies may hold hearings to discuss the preliminary budget requests. The result of the state-level review of the preliminary requests is the establishment of a budget request ceiling for the detailed asking budget. The budget ceiling is usually set by the governor's budget office and indicates the maximum request the governor might support in his or her budget message to the legislature six months prior to the beginning of the fiscal year. The budget ceiling then becomes an important part of the framework within which the institutions prepare their detailed asking budgets.

In states without formal preliminary asking budget cycles, the institutions, multicampus system offices, and state agencies arrive at a framework through informal discussions and negotiations. Normally, the state agencies, especially the governor's budget office and the legislative fiscal staff(s), communicate a budget ceiling or a range within which institutional requests will be accepted. State agencies also provide policy guidance on statewide issues such as productivity increases, state-level spending priorities, changes in accounting and purchasing structures, and proposed reallocations among public services.

Budget instructions and preparation of the budget request. The preparation of budget instructions and the assembly of departmental budget requests in public institutions are similar to those functions in independent colleges and universities.

Institutional review of budget requests. The review of budget requests in independent and public institutions is also similar. In the public sector, budget requests are usually prepared and reviewed between twelve to eight months before the fiscal year begins.

Budgeters in public institutions are under somewhat less pressure than their counterparts in independent institutions to provide regular projections of revenue for the coming fiscal year. The difference results in large part from the fact that state appropriations at levels reasonably close to the current and previous years are more or less assured, except, of course, when the state experiences serious economic difficulties. A major part of the analytical work of budget review is projecting enrollments and tuition and fee income on the basis of alternative tuition schedules. (Tuition and fee income is significant in that it tends to make up most of the difference between anticipated expenditures and state appropriations; it provides some "flexible" resources for the institution.) As in the independent sector, budgeters project student financial aid needs using alternative tuition and fees plans. Budgeters in public institutions that have large research programs or large endowments and annual gift programs, or both, regularly estimate the expected revenues from these sources, too.

In states that have some form of preliminary asking budget cycle, the review of budgets at the institutional level tends to be perfunctory, focusing on the mechanical aspects of budgeting (because the major policy issues are addressed in the preliminary cycle). In these situations budget review is normally performed by budget office staff and does not entail the wide-ranging participation of advisory groups.

Multicampus system, consolidated governing board, or segmental board review of budget requests. Institutions that are not part of a multicampus or segmental system typically forward their budget requests to the governing board nine to seven months before the fiscal year begins. Review by the governing board is similar to review by the board of trustees in the independent sector.

Budget requests from institutions that are part of a multicampus system, consolidated governing board system, or segmental system are reviewed by the central system or board staffs prior to being forwarded to the governing board. Whether or not the state has a preliminary asking budget cycle, most central system administrations conduct some form of preliminary budget request exercise. Program and activity priorities for the system campuses are established at this time. Accordingly, staff reviews of individual institutional requests are usually routine checks to ensure that the requests conform with system priorities and are assembled in the proper format.

An important role of the system-level review is the packaging of the request for presentation to the state agencies. Depending on statutory requirements or custom, the consolidated budget request may or may not identify individual campuses, though it usually identifies issues of systemwide importance, including faculty salaries; support for libraries; the cost of high-technology programs such as engineering, computer science, and the physical sciences; and problems arising from deferred maintenance. These priority issues are often presented independent of enrollment-related requests for resources. The level of sophistication of budget review and analysis is related to staff professionalization, experience, and size.

State agencies' review of budget requests. The routing of institutional budget requests at the state level differs from state to state depending on the role of each agency. Institutional requests are usually forwarded nine to seven months before the fiscal year begins. If the state higher education coordinating agency has very strong budget review powers, it may be the sole recipient of institutional requests. In that case the governor's budget office likely receives information copies and awaits the coordinating agency's recommendations. Legislative fiscal staffs may or may not receive information copies at this time. In states where the coordinating agency has weak budget review authority or is advisory on budget issues, the budget requests are normally forwarded to the governor's budget office with information copies sent to the coordinating agency.

Because several agencies are often involved in budget review at the state level, there is frequently considerable redundancy in the review process. In some states this redundancy leads to increased competition among the staffs. Perhaps the most noteworthy trend at the state level is that legislative fiscal staffs, and some governors' budget staffs, have grown rapidly in size and sophistication over the past two decades. The result is that in certain instances the budget role of state higher education coordinating agencies is being diminished.

Agencies generally review budget requests in the context of statewide master plans for higher education, enrollment targets for institutions, funding inequities among institutions, state financial conditions, and funding formulas or guidelines. Of all the agencies at the state level, the coordinating agency usually performs the closest examination of the relationship between major programs and activities and levels of funding. As at the system level, the degree of sophistication of analysis is tied to staff size and experience and the amount of time the agency is given for budget review. Coordinating agencies often have at most one month to analyze requests and make recommendations, normally conducting formal or informal budget hearings at which institutional representatives present their budget requests. Staff review may involve advisory councils of campus faculty and administrators.

The role of the coordinating agency, as perceived by other state-level agencies, varies from state to state. In some states it is seen as an advocate of higher education; in others it is viewed as a protector of state interests and hence a "cutter" of institutional budget requests. Most coordinating agencies strive to maintain what is perceived to be a neutral role between the institutions and other state agencies.

The coordinating agency staff make budget recommendations to the board or council, which in turn makes recommendations to the governor's budget office and the legislative fiscal staff(s). In states where the coordinating agency has strong budget review powers or where considerable trust exists between the coordinating agency and the governor's budget office, the coordinating agency's recommendations may be adopted without significant change. The governor's budget office staff generally examine the budget requests in relation to state revenue projections, enrollment targets, and funding formulas or guidelines. The more sophisticated budget office staff may examine programs and activities in greater detail by evaluating them on the basis of productivity or outcome measures, while the less sophisticated staff may examine line-item details without giving much attention to the institution's overall program plans. Frequently there is considerable communication between the governor's budget office and the institutions as the analytical work proceeds. However, the flow of information tends to be one-sided as the budget office seeks explanations or additional data to substantiate the institutional requests.

Typically, the executive budget office reviews budgets nine to six months before the fiscal year begins. The recommendations are reviewed by the governor and his or her chief aides and become part of the governor's budget message to the legislature and state. In many states the governor presents the proposed budget in January.

Legislative review of the governor's budget usually takes place between January and April, when the legislature is in session, although in some states the legislature does not convene until late spring. The character of the state legislature and its fiscal staff determines the nature of legislative budget review. Some states, such as California, have full-time legislatures that meet throughout the year. These states tend to have large and experienced full-time legislative fiscal staff. In many states legislators are part-time, meeting for sessions of 30, 60, or 90 days. Most of these legislatures have some permanent staff members to provide continuity and to support legislative committee activities when the legislature is not in session. In highly political states such as Illinois and New York, the minority and majority parties of each house have their own fiscal staffs; other states have a single legislative fiscal staff. The larger legislative fiscal staffs tend to be more sophisticated in terms of program and fiscal review because staff members are allowed to specialize.

Legislative fiscal staffs generally review budget requests while the legislature is in session. In those states where the legislature receives information copies of institutional requests, staff conduct preliminary analyses, often working directly or indirectly for the finance and appropriations committees, which hold budget hearings with all state agencies. Higher education's interests may be represented by officials from the state higher education coordinating agency, the consolidated governing board, the central system office, or the institutions. There is also considerable informal lobbying between individual institutions, system officials, and trustees on the one hand and legislators on the other. The legislative budget process is further complicated by committee actions, which often affect the level of appropriations.

Higher education is often one of the last appropriation items dealt with by the legislature and hence is more subject to fluctuations in the availability of state funds and to changes in the levels of other social services. The reason for this is that an increasingly large percentage of state activities is supported on an entitlement basis, whereby funding is set by statute and dictated by the level of demand for services or the volume of activity. Because higher education appropriations can be adjusted without statutory constraint, they can be treated on a discretionary basis. As J. Kent Caruthers and Melvin Orwig note, "Appropriations for higher education are determined in part on the basis of the need described in the budget request and in part on the basis of what resources are available after other state program commitments have been met."[4]

The discretionary nature of the higher education budget makes the setting of tuition and fees all the more important. In some states tuition and fees can be set by the institutions or by central system offices, thereby providing some flexibility in filling the gap between expected expenditures and the level of appropriations. In other states, tuition is formally set by institutional boards but informally controlled by the governor's budget office or the legislature. When tuition and fees are determined in large part by the executive budget office or legislative action, institutions lose flexibility.

Appropriations. Appropriations bills vary considerably from state to state. In some states, individual institutions are identified in the appropriations bill and receive direct appropriations; in others, resources are provided to systems or state postsecondary education agencies, which in turn distribute the funds to the institutions; and in others, appropriations are distributed by the governor's budget office.

The content of appropriations bills also varies widely. In some states certain kinds of revenues, such as tuition and fees, athletic fees, sponsored research, and auxiliary enterprises, are not included in the appropriations bill. Thus, the funds may go to the institutions without ever passing through the state treasury. Direct institutional control of these funds tends to afford the institution more flexibility in the use of its money. Moreover, some funds can be held in interest-bearing accounts.

The degree of detail in the appropriations bill often determines the extent of control exerted by state-level officials and agencies over institutional budgets and the amount of flexibility that institutions have in the use of appropriated resources. Generally, the potential for state-level control is greater as the number of program categories and line items, or objects of expenditure, in the appropriations bill increases.

In most states the appropriations bill also contains legislative directives, which specify legislative intent regarding certain issues. These riders may include cost-of-living and merit adjustments for faculty salaries, enrollment ceilings, expected tuition levels, funding levels for special programs not identified in the appropriations bill, or directions for the distribution of funds among institutions. In some states the governor has line-item veto authority after appropriation.

Allocation of appropriated funds. When funds are appropriated on a lump-sum basis to a system of institutions, the central administration must allocate the funds among the institutions. Similarly, when individual campuses receive their allocations, campus officials must distribute the funds among the various programs and activities. The distribution pattern will usually differ from the budget requests. Some resources will be removed to establish contingency funds to provide reserves in case of enrollment shortfalls or other emergencies. Reallocations may be made that alter the historical distribution of resources among institutions or among departments and support activities. Resources must be set aside, for example, for new instructional programs. Formulas used in some states to construct budget requests are normally not used by system and campus officials in allocating appropriated funds. Instead, allocations tend to be made on the basis of historical expenditures, enrollments, and assessments of programmatic need. Also, because so much of each budget is already committed to continuing activities, the reallocations have to be done at the margin.

Implementation of the budget. The expenditure of funds in public institutions is similar to the process in independent institutions.

Some states experience budget pressures after appropriations have been made and must make midcycle adjustments. For example, if one or more state agencies have overspent their resources, deficiency appropriations can be made during the budget cycle if the state has sufficient reserves. A more common situation, however, is a shortfall in state revenues, making midyear cuts in budgets necessary.

Closing out the fiscal year. The difference between closing out the fiscal year in public institutions and doing so in independent institutions is largely one of timing. Whereas independent institutions often allow two months to complete the closing process, public institutions sometimes must accomplish the closing within several weeks of the end of the fiscal year.

As with independent institutions, public institutions are audited both internally and externally. The external auditors are either from the legislative audit staff or from private accounting firms with which the state has contracted.

The appearance in some states of a relatively new state agency—the program and management audit staff—has implications for higher education. These agencies are often attached to the legislative or executive branch and take their cues accordingly. In some states program or management audits are conducted by the executive or legislative branch fiscal audit staff as an adjunct to its more accustomed financial audit responsibilities. Program audit staffs conduct audits of state agency activities, including program management and performance, to determine if those activities are conducted efficiently and effectively. Such audits extend far beyond the traditional examinations of financial responsibility. Several state program audit groups have conducted audits of programs and activities in higher education, and the number of such reviews is increasing. As agency staff gain experience, they can be expected to ask more penetrating questions about the conduct of business in higher education.

For Further Reading

A good overview of the factors that influence budgeting and the different kinds of budgeting is the article by William F. Lasher and Deborah L. Greene, "College and University Budgeting: What Do We Know? What Do We Need to Know?" in John C. Smart, ed., *Higher Education: Handbook of Theory and Research*, Vol. IX (Edison, NJ: Agathon Press, 1993). See also J. Kent Caruthers and Melvin Orwig, *Budgeting for Higher Education*, AAHE/ERIC Higher Education Research Report no. 3 (Washington, DC: American Association for Higher Education, 1979).

For technical discussions of institutional budgeting, the reader is referred to sections of Deirdre M. Greene, ed., *College & University Business Administration* 5th ed. (Washington, DC: National Association of College and University Business Officers, 1992).

Although the study was done nearly two decades ago, a two-volume report on a Princeton University project supported by the Ford Foundation is still an excellent case examination of institutional budgeting: *Budgeting and Resource Allocation at Princeton University* (Princeton, NJ: Princeton University, 1972), and *Budgeting and Resource Allocation at Princeton University*, Vol. 2 (Princeton, NJ: Princeton University, 1979).

The monograph by Hans H. Jenny (with Geoffrey C. Hughes and Richard D. Devine), *Hang-Gliding, or Looking for an Updraft: A Study of College and University Finance in the 1980s—The Capital Margin* (Wooster, OH, and Boulder, CO: The College of Wooster and John Minter Associates, 1981) is an excellent discussion of the relationship of capital budgets to annual operating budgets.

An overview of issues related to the budget process at the state level is presented by Daniel T. Layzell and Jan W. Lyddon, *Budgeting for Higher Education at the State Level: Enigma, Paradox, and Ritual*, ASHE/ERIC Higher Education Report 4 (Washington, DC: The George Washington University, 1990). A useful collection of essays on state-level and institutional-level budgeting is found in Larry L. Leslie, ed., *Responding to New Realities in Funding*, New Directions for Institutional Research no. 43 (San Francisco: Jossey-Bass, Inc., 1984). See also Anthony W. Morgan, "The Politics and Policies of Selective Funding: The Case of State-Level Quality Incentives," *The Review of Higher Education 15, no. 3* (Spring 1992): 289–306.

Notes

1. Aaron Wildavsky, *Budgeting: A Comparative Theory of Budgetary Processes* (Boston: Little, Brown & Co, 1979), p. 16.
2. Ibid., p. 161.
3. Association of Governing Boards of Universities and Colleges and the National Association of College and University Business Officers, *Financial Responsibilities of Governing Boards of Colleges and Universities* (Washington: AGB and NACUBO, 1979), p. 56.
4. J. Kent Caruthers and Melvin Orwig, *Budgeting in Higher Education*, AAHE/ERIC Higher Education Research Report no. 3 (Washington, DC: American Association for Higher Education, 1979), pp. 65–66.

FOUR
Allocating Resources and Increasing Flexibility
Working Within the Budget System

One question frequently asked about budgeting is "How can a participant effect change in the budget through the process?" In other words, "How does one change the pattern of budget allocations?" Specific questions can be asked about the process itself (e.g., Who should participate at each stage of the process? Does the budget follow from a strategic academic plan? What information is most useful to participants? How can the timing be adjusted to allow for more complete analyses?), or about the substance of budget decisions (e.g., How much should tuition and fees be increased? How large an increase should the various departments receive next year?). Over time, participants become more adept at phrasing and raising the questions so that they have the most impact possible.

Another frequently asked question, especially by those with day-to-day responsibility for budget planning and budget management, is, "How do I position my resources to maintain the most flexibility?" Flexibility is needed to accommodate change, which is inevitable. Contingency is a part of flexibility. Telephone rates increase midyear, steam lines break, faculty offered positions at other institutions need counteroffers, a distinguished faculty member at another institution wishes to relocate—these are examples of unanticipated events that can throw a resource plan off balance. Maneuverability is also a part of flexibility. This may mean that the funds with the fewest restrictions on their use are held so they can be applied against the greatest number of potential uses. State general funds usually cannot be used for construction projects larger than a certain threshold, whereas unrestricted gift money or interest earned on certain fund balances can be used for those projects. Flexibility comes from allocating state general funds for operating expenses, and directing gift or interest money to capital projects.

Another important question is "How much risk is tolerable?" A budget designed for flexibility and maneuverability is also intended to reduce risk. Risk can be gauged by the tolerances built into estimates of revenue, for example. The overcommitment of resources, with the expectation that some planned expenditures will not be made, can signal a budget with high risk.

Influence in the budget process is linked to certain decision points in the process. To wield influence, one may have to participate in those decisions that affect the most important resources or that are crucial for setting the resource environment for the institution.

Participants in the budget process generally expect that they can affect the way in which resources are distributed if they analyze their programs and activities in a logical, orderly manner. The issues raised in this chapter provide a framework for analytical thinking. However, the role of "politics" cannot be overlooked or underestimated in weighing budget outcomes. The political environment or the "spheres of influence" of members of the academic community vary from institution to institution. Through friendships with trustees or legislators, a dean, for example, may have political connections that provide him or her with influence far beyond the position. An administrator or faculty member who has participated in the budget process over many years may gain a knowledge of the institution and a collection of political debts sufficient to make him or her a powerful figure in budget negotiations. Some actors in the process are more articulate spokespersons than others and are more successful in acquiring resources. In general, the more complex the budget process and the interconnections among the actors, the more complex the political environment becomes. The framework presented in this chapter shows how institutions can strike a balance between rational planning and the inevitable political maneuvering.

This chapter identifies issues common to most colleges and universities that affect the distribution of resources, and suggests at which stages in the budget process these issues are typically addressed. It examines the sources of budget flexibility and discusses three decision points that have universal applicability:

☐   the academic plan;

☐ the allocation of faculty positions; and
☐ the enrollment plan.

   The first section of this chapter returns to the concept of institutional character. The second section covers the importance and the sources of budget flexibility, an assessment that usually occurs within a fiscal year. The third section examines the key decision points in the budget process; it reviews academic, administrative, and revenue factors that can be adjusted to alter the distribution of resources and suggests ways for faculty and administrators to question the basic assumptions upon which budgets are assembled. It includes a discussion of the potential hidden costs of administrative and programmatic decisions and examines administrative and revenue factors outside the institution that shape the budget. Institutional actors often have unrealistic expectations about affecting the process beyond the institution or inappropriate strategies for influencing higher-level decision makers.
   After key decision points are considered, the issue of "influence" is discussed. Questions about the resource allocation process at the institutional level address four areas: the budget process itself, academic and administrative policies and procedures, revenue estimation techniques, and the hidden costs of some activities. The final section covers some of the strategies used by decision makers to determine how to allocate resources in a flexible manner.

Institutional Character: The Environmental Factors

   As described in chapter 3, institutional character is an amalgam of variables depicting an institution's unique qualities. Institutional character is often driven by inertia, primarily because of historical tradition and the propensity of most organizations to change slowly. Accordingly, participants in the budget process cannot expect significant adjustments in the internal and external perceptions of the institution's character in a given budget cycle. For example, during the economic downturn experienced by many states in the early 1990s, faculty at public research universities were called upon to increase time devoted to undergraduate teaching by reducing their time spent on research. Because these universities achieved their reputations in large part through their research programs, and argued that there was a strong link between instruction and research, they did not wish to reduce their commitment to research. Although attention to undergraduate instruction generally has increased at these institutions, it has come through curricular and programmatic changes rather than through a diminishment of the research agenda.

In fact, the causal relationship is probably circular: institutional character changes slowly over time as a result of changes in the distribution of resources, and the allocation of resources may be adjusted to reflect the desire for a different institutional character. It is important to note that these relationships are loosely articulated: character does not respond immediately to changes, however major, in funding patterns.

However, there are occasions in an organization's "saga," as Burton Clark defines the collective understanding of the unique accomplishments in a formal organization, when the character can change dramatically.[1] Participants in the budget process who recognize these transition periods can strongly influence changes in institutional character and the allocation of resources. Clark identifies three settings for important changes in the development of organizational sagas or institutional character. The first and most obvious setting is the creation of a new institution. The second setting is what Clark characterizes as a "crisis of decay," during which the institutional community must decide whether to abandon the established behavior or allow the institution to fail. Today this situation is often marked by a change in leadership or a financial crisis brought about by a deteriorating economy, uncontrollable expenses, or plummeting enrollments. In the third setting the institution is ready for evolutionary change, a state difficult to discern because the institution is not in a crisis situation or a steep decline.

One indicator of possible change in institutional character is shifts in enrollment distribution among the disciplines. During the late 1970s and early 1980s, students tended to move from the liberal arts and social sciences to business and management and the physical sciences to pursue degrees having greater marketability. (In the 1990s we may see these patterns reversed as demographers, economists, and policy makers project a surplus of students trained in the physical sciences.) Pronounced changes in student preferences can force budgeters to shift faculty and staff resources to accommodate the new demands. Budgeters must determine whether enrollment shifts indicate short-lived trends or long-term changes in direction and then must decide whether to accommodate these shifts. Participants in the framing of institutional priorities, generally through the academic planning process, will be every bit as influential as those involved in the budget process. A new pattern of enrollments evolving over a short period of time may eventually change the character of the institution. Clearly, this kind of change is more likely at smaller institutions and at independent institutions, which have more control over their own destinies than public institutions. If, for example, faculty are to have a major role in shaping their institution's character, they will have to participate in reviewing the implications of enrollment projections.

A second indicator of change in institutional character is the composition of the faculty (in terms, for example, of age, training, disciplines, salaries, and scholarly productivity). From the late 1970s to the present, institutions generally have enjoyed a buyer's market for faculty in many disciplines. However, the needs and expectations of new faculty are often different from those of continuing faculty. With the number of faculty vacancies declining, the market in many disciplines has seen an abundance of talented young faculty who, though well trained as researchers, have often been employed by institutions whose primary mission is instruction. This can produce misalignment between mission and faculty expertise and expectations. For example, when a sufficient number of these bright, talented, research-oriented faculty arrive on a campus that does not have a strong research mission, there is strong pressure to strengthen the research component. These faculty owe their primary allegiance to their disciplines and realize that to maintain their stature in the profession and to ensure their mobility, they must continue active research. Altering the balance between teaching and research can affect the character of the institution over time.

A third indicator is financial condition, particularly in the case of independent institutions. Through careful management of resources and the generosity of alumni and other donors, some colleges and universities have accumulated a significant endowment or a working reserve (as opposed to restricted funds) that could serve as the foundation for a new mission.

A fourth indicator is the perception of the institution held by influential people, including legislators, members of Congress, powerful alumni, political figures, and special-interest groups. When influential outsiders believe that the institution has been of some benefit to them, they are more willing to provide financial or political support. Conversely, when these outsiders perceive that the institution has eroded their position or has not performed satisfactorily, they can lend their weight to an effort to limit resources. Except in crisis situations such as student disturbances or well-publicized confrontations between faculty and administrators, these changes in outside perceptions are slow to accrue. However, incidents can confirm notions, and notions build on one another to create perceptions of institutional character that dictate the behavior of influential people.

Significant changes in key indicators can lead to broad readjustments in the pattern of resource allocation. Thus, it is useful for budgeters to analyze their institution's character and estimate its place in the organization's saga. Because noteworthy upheavals in institutional character are generally limited, it seems more practical for budget participants to examine a number of academic, administrative, and revenue factors over which they have much more control on a year-to-year basis. These factors tend to be more tangible and, therefore, more subject to adjustment. The cumulative effect of these adjustments will be an alteration of the institution's character.

The Notion of Budget Flexibility

Unforeseen circumstances will likely shape the outcomes of most planning. Participants in the budget process must anticipate both disruptions in plans and the possibility of opportunities by incorporating alternatives into budget plans. A mark of a well-regarded institution is its ability to take advantage of opportunities and to respond to unanticipated problems. To influence the budgetary process on a day-to-day basis, budgeters must plan to have as much flexibility as possible in the amounts and availability of resources.

The experienced budgeter attempts to build as much flexibility as possible into the budget at every level of the process. Flexibility is defined here as a pool of resources that an individual can use for any purpose or as the ability to manipulate policies and procedures to alter outcomes. In a college or university budget, that pool of resources is usually extremely difficult to obtain or structure because of the heavy demands placed on available resources and the relatively autonomous functioning of departments and activities.

Personnel costs (salaries and wages and associated benefits for all employees) account for approximately 65 to 80 percent of most college or university budgets; fixed expenses such as utilities or maintenance represent approximately 10 to 15 percent. The balance is usually allocated to operating expenses such as service contracts, supplies, communication, noncapital equipment, and travel. Flexibility is usually structured according to the portion of the budget to which it pertains. Typically, restrictions on the uses of funds differ from one expenditure category to another. For example, in many institutions salary and wage money cannot be expended for operating or fixed expenses, but operating and fixed funds can be used for salaries and wages. Strategies for obtaining flexibility tend to be tailored to the function, to the expenditure restrictions affecting the institution, and to the level of operation within the institution.

In some circles the notion of flexible resources has the negative connotations of inefficiency and poor administration. Slack in an institutional budget is sometimes erroneously equated to "fat." One extension of this philosophy is the idea that a leaner budget translates into greater accountability. In fact, the most effective organizations tend to be those in which resources can be marshaled as necessary to meet contingencies and to take advantage of opportunities. Most budgeters guard against intrusions on their slack resources from both above and below in the organization's hierarchy.

Many persons in organizations have a natural tendency to want to shift uncertainty to other persons within the organization. Often department chairpersons, for example, depend over time on deans or campus-level administrators to provide resources for emergencies and opportunities, such as the overexpenditure of operating expense accounts, the costs of faculty hired on short notice to replace ill or incapacitated faculty, and the hiring of an excellent faculty candidate who recently appeared on the market. Responsibility for uncertainties that arise in departmental operations is thereby shifted to the dean or campus-level administrator. Similarly, deans and college-level administrators may closely monitor departmental spending to anticipate problems, or they may establish a reserve of funds to service departmental requests. In public systems of higher education, state-level officials shift uncertainty to system-level or campus-level administrators through statutes mandating that state agencies will not operate at a deficit.

The notion of flexibility changes from one budget cycle to the next as circumstances change. Sources of slack resources must change to adapt to new conditions, as must the strategies employed to obtain the slack. Although budgeters at all levels in the organization seek slack resources, they are naturally reluctant to identify those reserves to other institutional actors for fear of losing them.

Budgeters build flexibility into their plans in anticipation of significant changes in revenue or expenditures. (Although an unanticipated windfall of funds is a relatively infrequent occurrence, a savvy budgeter will know in advance how to shepherd such resources wisely.) These changes arise from four primary sources:

- enrollment fluctuations;
- revenue fluctuations;
- emergencies; and
- unforeseen opportunities.

The uncertainty surrounding enrollment projections is a major reason for building slack into the budget. If anticipated enrollments fail to materialize, a college or university loses tuition income or state appropriations or both. Unless reserve resources exist to cover the shortfall, the institution will have a deficit budget for that year. Similarly, enrollments above expectations can sometimes burden an institution's budget, even when the extra tuition income is considered, in that extra instructional sections may have to be scheduled with marginal registrations. Enrollments among degree programs may also shift so rapidly that it is not possible to reallocate resources, thereby creating an imbalance of teaching resources and requiring the staffing of additional instructional sections with temporary faculty.

Revenue shortfalls from sources other than tuition and fees will also unsettle an institution's budget. Endowment income may be less than projected because of a decline in the stock market or reversals in real estate investments. An economic downturn may mean that state income is less than projected, thereby leading to reductions in appropriations to public institutions. To meet anticipated revenue shortfalls, a state might impose higher budgetary savings targets. Revenue deficiencies also can be created when units overspend their budgets, usually because of poor fiscal management or inadequate fiscal information and controls, but also because of emergencies.

The range of emergencies for which resource reserves are needed is broad. For example, changes in federal student aid policies may place more of the burden of financial assistance on colleges and universities. The federal government may increase the minimum wage base for hourly employees. Soaring prices for gas and oil can send utilities expenditures higher than projected. An especially bitter winter or unseasonably hot spring or autumn can also undermine a utilities budget. If an institution is self-insured or has high deductibles, it might have to absorb significant losses arising from fires, severe storms, theft, or vandalism. Major building systems, such as heating and cooling, plumbing, and electrical networks, eventually deteriorate and have to be replaced, sometimes ahead of schedule. A roof or plumbing leak might cause extensive damage to sensitive equipment, personal articles, or building structure. Typically, these events cannot be anticipated when the budget is planned, some six to eighteen months prior to the beginning of the fiscal year. The best that budgeters can hope for is to set aside sufficient financial reserves or to be relatively free to alter other budget plans to accommodate the contingencies.

Ultimately, flexible funds have their origin in any revenue source: tuition and fee income, unrestricted endowment income, some state appropriations, unrestricted gift income, indirect cost recoveries from sponsored programs, and excess income from auxiliary and self-supporting activities. What is more important, is how reserves can be created and held free of the day-to-day demands of institutional operations. Strategies for the creation of resource reserves are discussed below. The strategies themselves are shaped in large part by the key decision points in an institution's budget process.

Decision Points

Influencing the budget process can be viewed from two complementary perspectives: the identification of key decision points in the process, whereby the budgeter can participate at critical junctures in the process with the smallest investment of time and effort; and the development of an arsenal of strategies that provide the budgeter with as much flexibility as possible. There are three decision points—the institution's academic plan, the allocation of faculty positions, and the institution's enrollment plan—at which a participant can directly influence the budgeting process at most institutions.

Academic Plan

In the best of circumstances, decisions concerning the allocation of resources are guided by program priorities. Those priorities are usually arrayed in an institution's academic plan or strategic plan. Priorities for support activities flow from the academic priorities.

Academic planning is conducted according to a very different timetable and process than budgeting, sometimes causing the linkage between the two to be elusive. Budgeting is cyclical, following the predictable schedule outlined in chapter 3. Academic planning is usually performed periodically, and initiated when it seems appropriate to re-establish program priorities and to set the institution's direction. The time required to complete an academic plan often extends beyond one budget cycle. Thus, it is difficult to link the two processes temporally.

Different members of the campus community often participate in the academic planning process as compared with those who participate in budgeting. Although overlap between the two processes in terms of people is ideal, so that budgeters will better understand program priorities and their origin, this is the exception and not the rule.

Academic planning requires divergent thinking, whereby different program options are explored and priorities are established. Budgeting requires convergent thinking, in that program priorities are matched to available resources. In addition, academic planning horizons are usually longer than budgeting horizons. Budgeting generally focuses on the fiscal year or biennium, while the academic plan often extends its perspective to a minimum of five years.

The linkage between academic planning and budgeting should come from the use of the product of the planning process—the academic plan—to serve as the framework for budget decisions. Academic plans differ widely in their specificity. Sometimes an institution with a broad, generalized academic plan will use a strategic plan to map the details of implementation for the near future. In any case, the academic plan indicates what is important, and hence what deserves resources.

Thus, to participate in the academic planning process is to be indirectly involved in the budget process. More important, however, the academic plan directs budget decisions. Because the academic plan sets the framework for decisions about the allocation of resources, it becomes a significant decision point outside of the budget process. The academic plan is also useful for several budget cycles. To exert influence over the budget process for a number of years, a budgeter should try to participate in the development of an institution's academic plan.

Allocation of Faculty Positions

The single most important institutional resource is the faculty. Regardless of how an institution accounts for that resource—be it numbered positions with established salary levels or a lump sum of money that can be used to employ any number of faculty—the decision about the distribution of vacant faculty positions or dollars that can be earmarked for faculty hires is the most important decision that can be made about resources. The decision is even more significant if an allocation of support money (for support staff, supplies, communications, office equipment, etc.) accompanies each faculty position.

It is not uncommon for decisions about the allocation of faculty positions to be made outside of the budget process. Although the resources for faculty positions are included in the budget, decisions about faculty often occur at times that are dictated more by program changes, hiring opportunities, and the need to cover a portion of the curriculum left uncovered due to a faculty member's departure than by the budget cycle.

Before decision makers can allocate faculty positions (and perhaps support money), they must have a systematic way to establish positions. New faculty positions can be created only if additional revenues are available from endowments, state appropriations (usually linked directly to an increase in enrollments), increased tuition (either from increased enrollments or increases in tuition levels), or business enterprises. Existing positions can be vacated through the nonrenewal of contracts, denial of tenure, resignation, retirement, or death.

A hierarchy of decision-making authority for the allocation of faculty positions should be established within the institution. One model is for the chief executive officer or chief academic officer to be responsible for faculty positions in a pool that includes all new positions and all positions vacated by retirement and death. In this model, academic deans are responsible for all positions vacated by retirement, and department chairs are responsible for all positions vacated by decisions to deny tenure. Decisions are timed to fit recruitment schedules or the unexpected needs of academic programs rather than the budget cycle.

Enrollment Plan

Many institutional resources, especially in the instructional and student services arenas, are allocated in response to the number of students that must be served. Clearly, controlling the number of students and the distribution of those students by school, college, or program has an important influence in the distribution of resources. The more sophisticated and accurate the enrollment projection and enrollment management models are, the more control campus decision makers have over the allocation of resources.

The development of a campus enrollment plan, based on predictions of acceptance rates for applicants and continuation rates for current students, usually occurs on a different schedule than the budget process. The enrollment plan in the aggregate must be connected to the budget process in that estimates of student fee and tuition revenue and instructional workload demands must be reflected in the budget.

Shaping the Policy Environment for Budgeting

Participants

Many questions about the institutional budget process are concerned with the degree of involvement of the various actors. For example, who should be involved in the preparation of budget requests? At the campus level, the issue is whether to give departments a role in assembling the asking budget or to make budget preparation the responsibility of the campus budget staff. The answer will depend on the kind of expectations one wishes to encourage among departments. For example, if the institution will not have sufficient revenues to satisfy even a fraction of departmental requests for additional resources, it may not be wise to arouse departmental expectations through the preparation of an asking budget. On the other hand, if one views the budget process as a political process in which competing parties present their best arguments for scarce resources and bargain for those resources, it may be appropriate for departments to be actively involved. In this case, requests and justifications are based on information that might not otherwise become available to participants at later stages in the budget process. The decision to involve departments therefore has the disadvantage of raising expectations that perhaps cannot be met and the advantage of providing additional information about resource needs. As faculty become more aware of the constraints, their expectations become more realistic and the potential for building consensus grows.

Budget reviews can involve budget staff and administrators only, or selected faculty and students as well. Constituent groups take part in the review process through a variety of mechanisms, including advisory committees and budget hearings. When faculty or students participate, there is generally a formal procedure on campus for selecting individuals. The nature of the participation (e.g., advisory or decision making), the parts of the budget to be reviewed, and the timing of the review are usually specified. How each of these factors is addressed will influence the outcomes of the budget process. For example, the selection of faculty and student participants by democratic voting may yield individuals who are the most active politically but who are not necessarily the best judges of programs and activities.

Participants not involved in day-to-day budgeting generally need budget staff assistance for background information and analyses. The effectiveness of the participation tends to be a function of the knowledge and experience brought to the review by participants or by budget staff and the willingness and ability of budget officers to provide data in a form that will facilitate a thorough review.

Another factor that affects who participates is the nature of the specific portions of the budget being considered. Reviews that focus on budgets in the academic area may miss the important contributions of administrative and support service budgets. In turn, reviews that focus on individual departments may miss significant relationships among programs. The timing of participation and the amount of time allotted for review will influence the effectiveness of the participation. Participants need sufficient time to weigh the evidence and examine the consequences of alternative allocation patterns. Resulting recommendations will be more useful to policy makers at higher levels if they are available before decisions are made and approved by governing boards.

Participants may become frustrated if they believe that the time and effort expended are not adequately recognized by the actors to whom they make recommendations or provide advice. However, not involving the academic community guarantees the loss of potentially valuable knowledge and experience. Therefore, the structuring of participation entails a realistic appraisal of the costs and benefits to the institution and to those involved in budget review. At Indiana University, for example, a faculty chairperson of the campus budget affairs committee expressed doubt about the value of that committee's role because it did not deal with the most crucial issues: budget planning, salary allocation, and plans for increasing revenues.[2] Generally, additional time is required for satisfactory participation, often creating conflicts with budget deadlines.

The degree of openness in the review process will be determined in large part by the character of the institution. Colleges with small faculties and staffs and a strong sense of shared governance will probably have relatively open deliberations. Institutions that are large or that lack a participatory governance structure tend to have a more closed budget review. An open process is usually seen as more desirable, particularly by those who do not have an active role in budget review. There are trade-offs, however, in adopting one approach over another. The more open the process is, the more difficult it tends to be for budgeters to ask difficult questions about programs and activities and to negotiate over the allocation of resources. On the other hand, the criteria for distributing resources may be more widely debated and known if the process is open. The opposite tends to be true of more closed deliberations. If budgeters are willing to sacrifice the privacy of their deliberations for the sake of broader knowledge of review criteria, they generally have some assurance that the information will be communicated accurately to members of the academic community. Still, budget participants in large institutions often find that communication channels are unreliable and transmit distorted information. Similarly, the give-and-take of budget review can sometimes generate mixed signals, especially if negotiations occur over a long period of time.

The problem of openness was confronted several years ago by a large campus that is part of a multicampus state university system. A faculty-administration committee was examining the fiscal and academic implications of transferring one or more degree programs to another campus in the system. During the deliberations, the identities of the programs under examination were released with statements summarizing the negotiations up to that point. Although the faculty and administrators in each program were cooperating with the committee, the premature release of information about the review placed these individuals in an awkward position. Several faculty members drew on the support of strong external constituent groups to block further action. In one program, faculty with the most visibility quickly sought, and were offered, positions in industry or at other universities. The review committee eventually recommended that this much-weakened program be transferred to another campus in the system.

Steps should be taken to provide adequate information about the budget review process to lower levels in the decision hierarchy. Departments or colleges often submit their budget requests (i.e., asking budgets) in the late summer or early fall and receive little information about the requests until the final budget is approved by the legislature (in public institutions) or by the governing board (in independent institutions). That is, the departments or colleges do not know how successful their arguments are or how they are perceived by decision makers at higher levels. Departments that begin to make plans for the following year based on their budget request may be shocked in the spring to learn that their expectations far exceeded the resources actually allocated. The disparity between asking budgets and appropriated budgets is seemingly magnified in the public setting because legislative action tends to occur long after initial submission. In some institutions the budget office staff or the budget liaison in the office of the vice president for academic affairs provides departments with summaries of budget recommendations at each major step in the review cycle. In special cases the president or the vice president for academic affairs can commit resources to departments before the final allocation has been determined by the governing board or the legislature. If, for example, a department is hosting a major scholarly conference or undertaking a major student recruitment program, it needs some assurance that it will receive the resources necessary to accomplish the task. On a case-by-case basis, the chief executive officer or the chief academic officer may wish to risk the early commitment of funds to guarantee success. If the burden of these special early commitments is not excessive, the president should be able to adjust the final budget to cover the promises.

Academic and Administrative Policies, Procedures, and Institutional Practices

An important way to influence the pattern of budget allocations is to alter the policies and procedures that govern the allocation and expenditure of resources. Because personnel expenditures account for most of the budget, it makes sense to question first the manner in which faculty and staff are used.

A useful framework for considering changes in a budget takes into account three factors:

☐ increases or decreases resulting from inflation or deflation;
☐ increases or decreases in workload; and
☐ improvement in or erosion of the quality of a program or activity.

Inflation or deflation factors reflect changes in prices of goods and services, including cost-of-living adjustments to salaries and wages. Changes in faculty workload usually reflect changes in enrollment or demand for course offerings and changes in the number of courses and sections taught; changes in administrative and staff workload mean changes in the level of service provided. The third factor accounts for qualitative changes in programs and activities. A decision to increase average faculty workload might be made with the expectation that the quality of instruction or advising will decline. Similarly, it might be possible to increase faculty workload and maintain program quality by introducing technologies such as computers or television or new instructional modes. Applying the three factors to budget review enables decision makers to be more discriminating in adopting budget strategies and more accurate in projecting the consequences of those strategies.

Programmatic directions. The first step in questioning the budget is usually to identify major issues and establish priorities for academic and support programs and activities. This review is facilitated by using an academic plan as a framework. Generally, resources are allocated to encourage or promote certain kinds of activities according to the dictates of program priorities. If, for example, research is one such priority, academic departments that are successful in attracting external research funding may be rewarded through the allocation of additional salaries and wage funds to support faculty release time. If higher enrollments are the objective, academic departments that increase their enrollments may be allocated additional faculty positions. If the objective is to increase the use of seminars and the case-study approach, the physical plant operation may need additional funds to renovate classrooms for case-study classes and seminars. The budget becomes a vehicle for sending messages about how programs and activities are valued. The strategic planning process sets the values, however. Thus, active participation in the strategic planning process directly shapes the environment for budgeting.

As budgeters review program priorities, they also decide the means by which progress is to be measured. Typically, the measures are a balance of quantitative indexes (e.g., student-faculty ratios, student credit hours per FTE faculty member, square footage serviced per member of the janitorial staff) and qualitative indicators (e.g., the quality of a department's faculty, national reputation of a department, faculty contact with students, perceived service orientation of support units). Because not all measures can be quantified, budgeters balance quantitative evidence with judgment.

Each of the specific issues concerning policies and procedures discussed below is defined by three factors.

☐ The extent to which the quality of the activity or program is being improved

☐ The extent to which the activity is responding to an increase in workload

☐ The extent to which the mission of the activity is being diminished, expanded, or redirected

Teaching loads. A college or university's single most important resource is its faculty (or the support of faculty positions). In allocating resources to departments, most institutions use some measure of instructional load. Four of the most commonly used indicators are student-faculty ratios, average student credit hours per FTE faculty member, faculty contact hours (i.e., weekly time spent in the classroom), and number of courses taught. Departments that have heavier credit-hour loads have higher student-faculty ratios and generate on average more student credit hours per faculty member. To determine the policy implications of these ratios, one must also consider the effect of class size on teaching loads. Class size and instructional methodology will also dictate the relationship between faculty contact hours and student-faculty ratios. Generally, the indicators are best used only to ask questions about the instructional process in departments and not as the sole basis for allocating resources.

Departments that depend heavily on laboratory or studio instruction have lower ratios than departments that have large lectures or sections. Questions can be asked about the extent to which departments depend on labor-intensive instruction.

☐ Should they or can they offer more balance between laboratory instruction and large lectures?
☐ Does the discipline really need one-on-one instruction, as in the studio training of musicians?
☐ Do accreditation standards limit departments to certain instructional methodologies?
☐ Could educational technologies such as television or computer-assisted instruction be used to reduce labor-intensiveness to allow expanding programs to maintain quality?

In disciplines where student demand is rising, are there ways to serve the students without increasing the number of faculty positions? The seemingly obvious answer—to increase faculty teaching loads—is often insufficient. Controlling demand for instructor time calls for a careful examination of instructional methodologies, course and section scheduling, and options such as enrollment rationing. Colorado College, for example, had a point system by which students bid for courses with enrollment limits. The University of Maryland's College of Business and Management established a minimum grade-point average for a student's first two years as a requirement for admission to the business major, which was in great demand.

Individual faculty teaching loads both within and across departments often differ widely. Within a department the following questions that reflect policy options can be raised.

☐ Are faculty members with lighter teaching loads given reduced loads as a matter of policy because they are more active and productive as scholars?

☐ Are faculty teaching loads skewed by rank, with, for example, full professors teaching two courses per semester and assistant professors three?

☐ Do such teaching assignments penalize junior faculty members by making it more difficult for them to find time for research?

☐ Do faculty members with equivalent credit-hour productivity really have the same teaching load? That is, does one individual teach multiple sections of the same course, while the second teaches several different courses?

☐ Do some teach chiefly the courses they want to year after year, or is there rotation among the courses, especially the basic or service courses?

It is also particularly useful to compare the department's current status to its status at various periods in the past. Regarding the interdepartmental situation, one can ask the following questions.

☐ Do differences in average faculty teaching loads reflect differences in the reputation, quality, and quantity of scholarly activity in the departments?

☐ Is the leadership in some departments more aggressive than in others in terms of the adjustment of instructional workload patterns within the departments?

Inevitably, some will argue that any interdepartmental comparison is unfair because the base time period is wrong for their own department.

Course credits weighting factors. Faculty positions are frequently allocated on the basis of measures of instructional load (e.g., student credit hours taught, headcount enrollment, classroom contact hours, and number of courses taught). Typically, the measures are composed of elements weighted by level of instruction or level of student. The weights are usually larger for more advanced levels of instruction or levels of student to reflect the belief that instruction at advanced levels is more time-consuming for faculty, and hence more expensive. The relative difference among weights may also reflect institutional priorities in terms of the relative importance of instruction at different levels. For example, lower-level undergraduate courses might be weighted 1.0, upper-level undergraduate courses 1.5, graduate course work 2.0, and graduate research 3.0. These particular weights, which are somewhat arbitrary, assume that a faculty member requires twice as much effort to offer one credit hour of graduate course instruction as to offer one credit hour of lower-division undergraduate instruction, or that graduate course work is valued twice as highly as lower-division undergraduate course work from a resource perspective. Clearly, differences between disciplines exist with respect to the effort required to offer one credit hour of instruction at a given level. Nonetheless, the weights are usually applied uniformly across an institution.

If the weights used to compute teaching load are indicative of an institution's priorities, a change in weights signifies a change in priorities. If resources are allocated on the basis of weighted student credit hours, for example, a change in weights will lead to a change in the distribution of resources. Figure 4.1 illustrates that the weighting factors differ greatly across a select group of public institutions. From the range of values, and for a given distribution of "raw," or unweighted, credit hours, it is possible to develop a sense of the size of potential shifts in resources when weights are changed. Figure 4.2 illustrates the effect of altering the weighting scheme on two departments at the same institution. The department that has a larger share of its enrollments at the graduate level will be authorized a larger number of faculty positions as a result of introducing the richer weighting scheme.

Distribution of faculty ranks. Departments with a higher proportion of junior faculty tend to be "cheaper" to support because salaries are lower than in departments with a higher proportion of senior faculty. In addition to the fiscal implications of the distribution of faculty by age and rank, there are several academic concerns.

□   Is the distribution of faculty expertise within a discipline appropriate for both the department's instructional and research missions?
□   Is the proportion of tenured faculty sufficiently low to guarantee a flow of "new blood" into the department?

Figure 4.1   Student Credit Hour Weighting Factors Reported by AAU (Association of American Universities) Institutions, 1982–83

	Lower Division	Upper Division	Graduate Instruction	Graduate Research
California	1.0	1.5	2.5	3.5
Colorado[1]	1.0	1.8	3.6	4.7
Minnesota	1.0	1.0	1.5	1.5
Missouri	1.0	2.0	4.0	4.0
Nebraska	1.0	1.6	3.4	6.5
Oregon	1.0	2.0	4.0	4.0
Washington[2]	1.0	1.8	4.3	6.0
	1.67	2.86	4.3	6.0
Wisconsin	1.0	1.7	3.92	6.06

1. Based on average direct-cost dollars per student credit hour resulting from the Major Research Universities Information Exchange Project.

2. The higher weights are used for "high-cost" programs such as architecture and engineering.

Source: Private correspondence, Marilyn Brown, University of Maryland, College Park, 1983.

□   Conversely, should the quality of the experienced teacher be more fully recognized?

□   Do standards for tenure and promotion differ significantly among departments?

□   Should such standards differ when people of higher quality can be hired in some disciplines?

□   Are vacant positions filled at the same rank held by the former incumbent?

It should be noted that faculty demographics are often slower to change than institutional policies and procedures.

Figure 4.2 Faculty Staffing as Determined By Weighting Factors

(Assume 1.0 FTE faculty position carries a load of 600 weighted student credit hours.)

Dept A	Credit Hours by Level of Instruction	Weighted Weighting Factor		Student Credit Hours	
Lower division	3,000	1.0	[1.0]	3,000	[3,000]
Upper division	4,000	1.5	[1.5]	6,000	[6,000]
Graduate instruction	1,500	2.0	[2.5]	3,000	[3,750]
Graduate research	500	3.0	[3.5]	1,500	[1,750]
				13,500	[14,500]

$$\text{Number of full-time equivalent faculty positions} = \frac{13,500}{600} = 22.5$$

$$= \left[\frac{14,500}{600} = 24.2 \right]$$

Dept B

	Credit Hours by Level of Instruction	Weighted Weighting Factor		Student Credit Hours	
Lower division	2,000	1.0	[1.0]	2,000	[2,000]
Upper division	3,000	1.5	[1.5]	4,500	[4,500]
Graduate instruction	2,500	2.0	[2.5]	5,000	[6,250]
Graduate research	1,000	3.0	[3.5]	3,000	[3,500]
				14,500	[16,250]

$$\text{Number of full-time equivalent faculty positions} = \frac{14,500}{600} = 24.2$$

$$= \left[\frac{16,200}{600} = 27.1 \right]$$

Distribution of faculty salaries. The distribution of faculty salaries will vary from one department to another for a number of reasons, each of which in turn raises a question about budget policy.

☐ Does the distribution of faculty salaries follow closely the pattern of faculty ranks?

☐ Does the distribution of faculty salaries reflect more the seniority hierarchy or the contributions and professional accomplishments of the faculty?

☐ What are the incentives and disincentives that result?

☐ Has the salary difference between entering faculty and faculty with long service to the institution been compressed? If so, is this compression created by market conditions in disciplines such as business, engineering, and computer science?

☐ Do some departments fill vacant positions at ranks lower than those of former incumbents? Is this strategy necessitated by rapidly rising salaries in the market competition for new faculty?

☐ Do the differences in faculty salaries across disciplines accurately reflect the differences in the market for faculty?

The salary distribution issue frequently arises when a department seeks to fill a vacant faculty position, especially one in the senior ranks. One strategy has been to fill vacant senior professorial posts with junior faculty members. The oft-mentioned advantages of this strategy are that the difference in salaries can be used elsewhere in the department; there is more opportunity to promote junior faculty; and the department can use new talent. However, a department must consider the potential loss of senior leadership. A faculty that is relatively junior usually needs a core of senior faculty positions to provide leadership.

A question frequently raised by faculty is how to determine the size of faculty and staff salary adjustment pools each year. In the aggregate, salary adjustments depend heavily on the size of the increase in institutional income, which is largely derived from appropriations, endowment income, and tuition and fees. Generally, the total pool of resources available for salary adjustments is divided into two parts: one for merit adjustments, the other for across-the-board, or cost-of-living, adjustments. At some institutions a portion of the total salary adjustment pool is set aside as a contingency fund for special recruitment and retention needs or to pay for the upgrading of faculty positions resulting from promotions.

In public institutions, the cost-of-living adjustment as a percentage of base salary is frequently mandated for all public employees. There is no national pattern for the relative sizes of cost-of-living and merit adjustments. Ideally, the merit pool is considerably larger than the cost-of-living pool so that an individual's performance can be rewarded.

Typically, the merit adjustment pool allocated to each department or administrative unit is a percentage of total base salaries. If the chief executive officer, chief academic officer, or deans set aside a portion of the institution's total salary adjustment pool as a contingency fund, the pro rata departmental allocations may be supplemented to reflect differences among departments in terms of market conditions or institutional priorities.

Use of part-time and temporary faculty. As budgets become tighter, more departments and institutions depend on part-time and temporary faculty to make ends meet. Generally, a part-time or temporary faculty member receives less compensation on a course-by-course basis than a permanent faculty member. Also, part-time and temporary faculty can be employed as needed; when student demand shifts, part-time and temporary faculty can be hired or released to accommodate these shifts. One negative feature of part-time and temporary employment is that some individuals become academic gypsies, moving from one temporary position to another without the benefits received by permanent faculty. Accordingly, one would expect temporary faculty to be less committed to their institutions. Temporary faculty often receive heavier teaching assignments than permanent faculty, making it more difficult for them to pursue scholarly activities. Also, part-time faculty tend to be less available to students and colleagues because of their other obligations.

To employ part-time and temporary faculty, departments generally must use funds earmarked for adjunct faculty or funds from vacant faculty positions. However, some institutions have policies that prohibit using money from permanent faculty positions for temporary and part-time faculty. Institutions must consider the following questions.

☐ Should departments have the latitude to hold faculty positions purposely vacant to provide the resources for temporary hiring?
☐ Do large departments have enough faculty turnover or faculty on sabbatical leaves or leaves of absence without pay to generate funds for part-time and temporary faculty without having to hold positions vacant?
☐ Do undergraduates experience too large a proportion of their courses with temporary or part-time instructors?
☐ Do departments employ savings gained in the use of part-time and temporary faculty in the instructional area, or are those savings diverted to other activities such as departmental research and service?

Budgeters in public institutions often must be cautious in attempting to increase flexibility by using part-time and temporary faculty. In some states faculty positions that are vacant for more than one or two years are eliminated from the institution's budget. Other states closely monitor the number of FTE faculty employed, including part-time and temporary faculty, to ensure that the number does not exceed the budgeted faculty FTE count.

Sabbatical leaves. Many institutions have a sabbatical leave policy for faculty that provides individuals with one year of leave at half-salary or one semester at full salary for every six to ten years of full-time service. Some institutions award one-semester sabbaticals every seventh semester. For faculty leaves of one year, departments can use the salary saved to employ part-time instructors to cover the permanent instructor's courses and, if the permanent instructor's salary is sufficiently large, as funding for other activities. Generally, departments lose resources with sabbaticals of one semester at full pay because they must employ substitute instructors and at the same time pay the faculty member's entire compensation. Departments may vary considerably in the handling of sabbatical leaves. Budgeters should ask the following questions regarding sabbatical leaves.

☐ Are all faculty granted such leaves when they have met the minimum service requirement?
☐ Are faculty required to seek outside funding to cover part of the sabbatical leave?
☐ Are only year-long sabbatical leaves at half-salary permitted?
☐ If one-semester sabbaticals at full pay are permitted, are the absent faculty member's courses canceled or are temporary instructors employed to teach the courses?

Graduate assistants. In institutions that offer graduate-level instruction and have budgeted graduate assistant positions, departments may differ significantly in how the graduate assistants are used; graduate assistants are a source of considerable flexibility. The primary question to be addressed is how departments actually use their graduate assistants (i.e., the extent to which assistants are used as graders, instructors of independent sections, research assistants, or administrative aides). Another issue is the basis on which graduate assistant positions are allocated to faculty—seniority, the percentage of teaching load made up of large lecture classes, or scholarly and research productivity. Assistant positions could also be granted across-the-board.

Support staff. The distribution of support staff (e.g., bookkeepers, secretaries, laboratory technicians) may vary a great deal from department to department. Are differences the result of specific instructional methodologies, the nature and extent of research activities, instructional loads, service commitments, or simply historical evolution? To what extent should support staffing be adjusted among departments? To what extent can investments in new technologies such as desktop publishing and computerized accounting systems reduce the need for support staff?

Administrative and student support. The academic portion of the institutional budget cannot be understood without analyzing its relationship to the administrative and student support budgets. If one assumes that the academic mission (i.e., instruction, research, and service) is primary, academic and student support budgets could be expected to be developed to facilitate operations in the academic arena. As happens in most organizations, however, the support operations can sometimes take on lives of their own. Many campuses have policies calling for periodic review of the effectiveness of such operations. The reviews are excellent vehicles for raising and studying budget questions.

Following are some of the many questions that could be asked about support operations.

- ☐ Is this service essential to the campus?
- ☐ Is there a duplication of services on campus?
- ☐ To what extent are new technologies (e.g., computerized accounting, personnel, payroll, and data systems; desktop publishing; energy monitoring systems) being used to reduce the number of staff required and to make operations more efficient?

For auxiliary enterprises, the following questions arise.

- ☐ Are the activities fully self-supporting?
- ☐ Do they pay their fair share of costs for space, utilities, maintenance, accounting services, and the like?

In examining the physical plant operation, one can ask the following questions.

□ Is the salary structure competitive with market conditions in the area?
□ Has this affected the frequency of vacancies?
□ What steps have been taken to conserve energy in campus facilities?
□ How much would it cost to upgrade campus facilities to achieve significant savings in energy usage?
□ Does the physical plant operation follow a plan of preventive maintenance for campus facilities?
□ What are the long-term costs of deferred maintenance?

In the student affairs operation, one can question the extent to which policies concerning the availability of on-campus student housing influence student enrollment, student retention, and the character of the institution. The fiscal and academic implications of policies regarding a nonacademic operation on campus are illustrated by the experience of a large university located near a major urban center. This institution has a strong commuter orientation. Students and faculty tend to pursue their cultural and social activities away from campus; accordingly, the campus is not perceived to offer much of a sense of intellectual community. Preference for on-campus student housing is given to upperclassmen; freshmen are not guaranteed housing. This policy may discourage the development of a sense of community among freshmen. If freshmen are not encouraged to view the campus as an intellectual and social community, it is more difficult for them to change their impressions when they become sophomores, juniors, and seniors. Thus, a policy controlled by the student affairs office has important implications for the institution's academic environment. It is interesting to note that one reason the housing policy at this institution has not been altered is concern for a balanced budget. The student housing administrators have fiscal projection models that accurately predict revenues under the existing housing policy. If the policy were to change so that freshmen receive preference in on-campus housing, the fiscal models would have to be redesigned, and housing officials there have no historical database available for inserting new parameters into the models. Officials fear that they might lose money for several years until they are able to predict accurately residential patterns under a new housing policy. This short-run concern for avoiding risks is thus preventing officials from uplifting the intellectual and social environment of the campus. A willingness to invest resources to cover deficits that might occur during the transition could produce a major benefit in terms of a more positive attitude toward the institution on the part of students. This improved attitude would probably contribute to increased retention and would in the long run attract more students.

Operating expenses. Academic and support departments and activities can be evaluated in terms of how effectively they use their money for day-to-day operating expenses such as communications, travel, supplies, and equipment. The following questions can be asked of departments or faculty committees.

☐   Are faculty who are presenting papers or serving on panels the only ones to receive travel funds?
☐   Does the department or committee use a priority ranking of the discipline's various professional meetings to ration travel funds?
☐   In academic, administrative, and student support areas, are administrators and support staff who are presenting papers or attending workshops the only ones to receive travel funds?

Because excessive telephone charges can imperil any unit's budget, budgeters can ask what steps have been taken to subscribe to long-distance telephone services, to design a telephone system that is effective and relatively inexpensive, to monitor long-distance telephone calls and charge faculty for nonbusiness usage, and to disconnect grant-supported telephones when external support ceases. Most institutions have a central purchasing department that orders and stores routine supplies in bulk. Would it be cheaper for the institution to use several large-volume distributors rather than operating a campus-based central store? To what extent do departments purchase supplies on their own? Do departments take advantage of discounts on purchases of large quantities of supplies? When purchasing equipment, do departments seek educational discounts or prepayment discounts? Do departments take advantage of institutionwide low-cost maintenance agreements for standard pieces of equipment such as typewriters and computer terminals?

Number of budget cycles. The number of budget cycles influences the perspective brought to the budget process. Attention to one budget cycle, usually one fiscal year, generally focuses on the details of incremental changes from the current budget cycle. A horizon of two or more budget cycles permits the budget to become more a vehicle for planning. The further into the future the budget looks, the less budget detail is required (or can be expected). A long-term budget should highlight proposed changes in the relationship between programs or activities. If, for example, resources are intended to be reallocated from one academic program to another, a multiyear budget proposal can sketch the phasing of the shift of resources without requiring line-item detail for each of the future budget cycles.

Budget format. Another question about the process concerns the appropriateness of budget format. In public institutions, budget formats are dictated in large part by the requirements of state-level agencies. To reduce the burden of budget preparation within the institution, budgeters often develop their budgets in accordance with the specifications of those agencies. However, the kind of information required by state-level officials is often not useful to institutional decision makers.

An extreme example of the impact of budget formats was seen in Connecticut in the mid-1970s. State budgeters opted to change to a program budget format, maintaining a parallel flow of budget documentation in the old line-item (i.e., object of expenditure) format. Because most of the state budgeters were familiar with the line-item approach and did not understand how to frame their analyses around program formats, the program budget documents were collected but not used during the budget review stage.

State-level officials usually examine aggregate data that focus more on the institution as a whole than on individual departments or programs. It may be necessary for institutional budgeters to develop parallel budget formats that can be used more effectively for internal decision making.

In both the public and the independent sectors, it is appropriate to question the structure of the budget and the kinds of information contained therein. The picture of an institution will vary depending on whether budgets are constructed with object-of-expenditure detail, program categories for program budgeting, or decision packages for zero-base budgeting. Each format requires different information and forces budgeters to ask different kinds of questions about institutional activities. Similarly, does the budget include all revenue sources, or only state appropriations (public institutions) and tuition and endowment revenue (independent institutions)? In the public arena, especially in multicampus systems, it is common for money, often earmarked, to arrive on campus throughout the fiscal year. Unless all sources of revenue can be arranged against proposed expenditures in one document, or in a single process, it is difficult for participants to grasp the magnitude of the budget or to establish funding priorities effectively.

Revenue Sources

Budgets are shaped by available revenues, as well as by changes in academic and administrative policies and procedures. How revenues are projected and how institutional policies and procedures influence the availability of resources are important considerations to budgeters. In both the public and the independent sectors, student enrollments are probably the single most influential determinant of institutional income. Endowment income is a major consideration at only a few institutions in the U.S.; in 1993, only 294 colleges and universities had endowments exceeding $35 million.[3] Many institutions supplement their endowment income with gift revenues. A small number of institutions have sponsored research programs attracting hundreds of millions of dollars. Most of this money is restricted to the research activities themselves, however, and do not constitute a pool of revenues over which an institution has significant control. The major research universities do generate millions of dollars annually in overhead reimbursements used to fund staff and plant operation.

Enrollment projections. Projecting student enrollments is an art, not a science. An institution that projects enrollments accurately over time knows its potential audience and successfully controls a number of key variables, including acceptance rates, student retention rates, tuition levels, and the attractiveness of academic programs.

An institution's character will in large part define the potential population of students. Accordingly, an understanding of an institution's character will shape the kinds of questions raised.

☐ What is the target population, and what characteristics of the institution help define that population?

☐ Does the target population need to be expanded to obtain a larger pool of potential students?

☐ Would this expansion affect the quality of the student body?

☐ Are there some components of the institution's character (e.g., array of academic programs, student housing policies, athletic programs) that can be adjusted to make the institution more attractive to prospective applicants?

☐ Has the target population changed dramatically in recent years?

As the competition for students increases, some institutions are turning to aggressive advertising and recruitment campaigns. Because these can be quite expensive, budgeters usually weigh the costs against the benefits as measured by increased applications or growth in matriculations.

☐ Should the institution employ its own publicity staff, or should it contract for advertising services?

☐ What kind of advertising should be undertaken?

☐ To what audience should the advertising be directed?

☐ Should professional recruiters be hired by the institution?

☐ Can recruitment be done to some extent by students, faculty, and alumni?

Every institution has a pool of applicants, and that pool may overlap with pools of other institutions. Applicants are screened by an admissions office and perhaps by a faculty committee, which evaluate each candidate according to institutional entrance criteria. Because many potential students apply to more than one institution and some for various reasons decide not to enter college, a percentage of those admitted will not matriculate. Enrollment projections are usually based on a firm knowledge of the historical acceptance and matriculation rates and on the confidence that the projected rates will not differ from historical patterns. When radical changes are made in institutional character—such as when the institution becomes coeducational, or no longer requires students to live on campus, or changes its admissions criteria—or if economic conditions change markedly, the acceptance and matriculation rates cannot be projected from historical data. Also, enrollment projections must be adjusted to reflect the trend in average student load, which in recent years has been decreasing. Clearly, the number of matriculating students is crucial in that it will determine tuition revenue and, in most public institutions, state appropriations.

- ☐ If the number of candidates offered admission is too small, are admissions standards too strict?
- ☐ If the number of candidates offered admission is too large, are admissions standards too lax?
- ☐ If applicants are required to specify their proposed degree major, does the distribution of candidates offered admission resemble the distribution of faculty resources?
- ☐ To what extent will more attractive student aid packages help to improve acceptance and matriculation rates?
- ☐ If those rates fluctuate widely from year to year, should admissions standards be changed?
- ☐ Are life experiences credited in evaluating candidates for admission?
- ☐ What special requirements and obligations are associated with equal opportunity in the admissions process?
- ☐ Are transfer students encouraged to apply?
- ☐ Are admittance rates for transfer students adjusted to compensate for changes in the admittance rates of first-time students?
- ☐ Is course availability and scheduling a hindrance in students' progress toward their degrees?

Admissions to graduate programs are usually treated differently from admissions to undergraduate programs.

- ☐ Are admissions processed by an office of graduate studies or by individual departments?
- ☐ Does the office of graduate studies control the allocation of admissions slots by department and program?
- ☐ Who establishes the criteria for admission to graduate programs?
- ☐ Are the financial aid or graduate assistantship packages attractive to prospective students?

One aspect of enrollment projections is estimating the number of matriculated students who will continue at the institution until graduation. Over time a retention history evolves that is used to guide the projections. Students remain at or depart from institutions for any number of reasons. However, because it makes sense financially (and, one hopes, educationally) to retain as many students as possible, some institutions have introduced retention programs. Budgeters should ask several questions about those programs.

☐ Are they necessary?
☐ What is their cost and do the costs outweigh the gains?
☐ Financial gains can be estimated in terms of net revenue, that is, additional income from tuition and fees and charges for room and board less the incremental costs of financial aid, recruitment, housing, and food services. Are resources, and particularly new staff, needed so that faculty can be released from teaching and other obligations in order to assume more counseling and advising responsibilities? Or is it more appropriate to hire additional counselors to release faculty from advising assignments?
☐ What teaching loads will be imposed on faculty in particular departments and what burdens will be placed on administrative staff?

Tuition and financial aid. A key variable in the determination of net revenue is tuition less in-house financial aid to students. Tuition levels are typically established in close relationship with enrollment, revenue, and expenditure projections. Until the last five to ten years, tuition income roughly made up the gap between total estimated expenditures and the sum of other income. This gap was especially large in independent institutions. Few institutions have that kind of price-setting flexibility today. Setting tuition charges has become more complex than simply selecting a figure that will yield a balanced budget. Setting the tuition prices and aid levels is an interactive process between competing claims on resources, estimates on the return on investments, and imposed spending discipline. It is also frequently an agonizing process. The following questions should be asked when reviewing a potential tuition increase.

☐ To what extent will the tuition increase work to reduce enrollment, even with an increase in financial aid?
☐ At what point will the tuition increase actually reduce revenue?

- Should the tuition charged at competitive institutions be used as a benchmark in establishing new tuition levels?
- Should tuition vary by degree program or student class level to reflect the different costs of programs?
- What is the appropriate relationship between undergraduate and graduate tuition charges?
- Similarly, should financial aid be employed to adjust net charges to particular groups of students?

The calculation of net revenue per student is important for small institutions, where incremental increases or decreases in enrollment can determine the fate of faculty and staff positions and basic services.

Generally, student fee structures are considered with tuition charges. The setting of fees is a much murkier area than the setting of tuition levels because many fees (e.g., student housing, dining, parking) are earmarked for auxiliary enterprises, which are self-supporting, and student services. Budgeters can use the establishment of fee structures as a means to examine the financial operations of self-supporting programs. On many campuses, for example, student affairs activities such as intramural athletics, student government, and health clinics are budgeted largely through fees. A number of institutions charge for private music lessons, and others have a laboratory fee to generate income for academic departments that use laboratories in instruction. Some fees are charged to faculty and staff as well as to students. Income from parking fees, for example, might be used to maintain parking lots and campus roadways for the benefit of the entire academic community. In some public institutions it may be possible to increase fee levels proportionally more than tuition levels because of state oversight in the establishment of tuition. Thus, funding for academic programs might be slighted while student services or self-supporting activities flourish. Also, institutional advocates of low tuition may be unaware of proposed fee increases because tuition charges and fee charges are sometimes established through separate processes by different participants.

Endowment. Many actors in the budget process are not familiar with endowments, as these investments are often managed by a committee of the governing board, a separate development office, or professional investment counselors. Although budgeters generally need not concern themselves with the day-to-day management of endowments, they can raise questions about the direction of investment policies and the relationship between the policies and the revenue generated for the institution.

- How is the investment portfolio balanced to accommodate the need for capital growth on the one hand and operating income on the other? If the portfolio leans too heavily toward capital growth, it may produce insufficient income for the budget. If the portfolio leans too heavily toward income generation, it may not grow enough to keep pace with income needs and inflation.
- What is the rate of return on the investment portfolio?
- How does this compare with the returns for other kinds of portfolios?
- How should endowment income be defined?
- At what rate is income and growth from the endowment drawn down?
- How much income/capital gains should be retained to maintain purchasing power of the endowment?

A major policy decision that will influence revenues directly is determining the proportion of investment income allocated to the budget. Another series of questions can be raised about endowment income.

- Should it be used primarily to fund continuing activities, or as seed money for new activities?
- Should part of endowment income be set aside for contingencies?
- To what extent is endowment earmarked by donors for particular programs and activities?

Gifts. Most institutions receive more income from gifts than from endowment. Gifts are less predictable than endowment income unless an institution has an established record of receiving gifts and employs staff to pursue them actively.

- How cost-effective is the development staff? That is, how much more does the staff recover in gifts than is spent for salaries and operating expenses?
- Are there ways in which the institution can pursue gifts more aggressively so that income will be more predictable?

- Should the institution have an alumni office?
- For institutions with a religious affiliation, how steady a source of income is the church?

Research funding. In preparing the budget, institutions with substantial sponsored research activity normally project contract and grant revenues. By the early 1990s, for example, Stanford University had developed a reputation for aggressively pursuing charges for the indirect costs of research. This considerable dependence on income from indirect charges became a liability when the federal government began to question the appropriateness of some of the charges, and disallowed a significant number.

Historical information concerning the number of contract and grant applications made and the number funded is of questionable value because the priorities for federal research support change constantly in today's economic environment. Moreover, the federal government is seeking to place ceilings on charges for the indirect costs associated with research activity.

- What are the current federal priorities?
- Does the institution have research activity in those areas?
- What are the possibilities of joint research enterprises with business and industry?
- Are there private sources of funding, such as foundations, that might support sponsored programs?
- How much do indirect cost rates differ among sponsored activities such as training programs, laboratory research, or off-campus research?

Sponsored research can make a significant contribution to an institution's instructional program by covering part of the costs of graduate education. Research projects often involve graduate students as research assistants. A number of graduate students, especially in the physical and biological sciences, receive their research training this way. In addition, research funding often complements the institution's allocations to departments by providing additional funds for faculty travel, secretarial support, equipment purchases, and other items.

Accounting Standards

The financial condition of an institution is reported in financial statements that are prepared in accordance with generally accepted accounting principles established by designated governing bodies. The authoritative group for independent colleges and universities is the Financial Accounting Standards Board (FASB); the group for public institutions is the Governmental Accounting Standards Board (GASB). When these governing bodies change financial reporting procedures, the financial profile of institutions as depicted in financial statements can be transformed markedly. Budgeters need to understand how changes in financial statements affect the picture of institutional resources.

Recently FASB introduced two new standards, Statement of Financial Accounting Standards (SFAS) No. 116, *Accounting for Contributions Received and Contributions Made*, and SFAS No. 117, *Financial Statements of Not-for-Profit Organizations;* these will significantly change the financial statements for most independent colleges and universities in fiscal years ending on or after December 15, 1995. These changes, in turn, may cause people familiar with the previous formats and protocols to raise questions about institutional finances.

SFAS No. 116 establishes accounting standards for contributions received or made. Among the provisions are the following: defining a contribution; distinguishing contributions from other transactions such as exchanges or agency relationships; recognizing unconditional promises to give as contributions; distinguishing among contributions received that increase permanently restricted net assets, temporarily restricted net assets, and unrestricted net assets; and releasing restrictions on temporarily restricted net assets for operating activities. SFAS No. 116 introduces new terminology that budgeters must understand, such as the distinction between unconditional and conditional promises, and raises the issue that the determination of when a contribution is recognized in the financial statements is tied to the conditions of the donor. To be restricted, funds must apply to activities that are not part of the existing program of activities and services. For example, gifts that underwrite part of the operation of an academic unit or that are allocated to general financial aid could be construed as unrestricted. Similarly, gifts with stipulations that are satisfied within the course of the fiscal year in which they are received could also be considered unrestricted.

SFAS No. 117 establishes standards for external financial statements provided by not-for-profit organizations. It explains how to report assets, liabilities, net assets, revenues, expenses, gains, and losses. One intent of SFAS No. 117 is to simplify the nonprofit financial statement by mirroring the corporate model. The revised aggregated statement of financial position for independent institutions does away with the fund balance as it has been known in the past, replacing that section of the balance sheet with total net assets for the institution as a whole divided into three groups: unrestricted net assets, temporarily restricted net assets, and permanently restricted net assets. This format aggregates the detail that previously was distributed by fund group (i.e., current funds, loan funds, endowment funds, and plant funds, all further divided as to unrestricted, restricted, and in the case of plant funds, investment in plant).

The aggregation of financial data according to SFAS No. 117 may at first glance lead a budgeter to believe that an institution has more unrestricted funds than it had under previous accounting standards. However, more funds are carried as unrestricted in SFAS No. 117. For example, funds functioning as endowment and much of the gain on regular endowment may now appear as unrestricted new assets (reminiscent of the unrestricted current fund balance). Some members of the campus community will ask if this is a special reserve and will want to know why it cannot be spent. Similarly, many independent institutions will carry plant values as unrestricted funds. Depreciation, which under the previous model was a deduction from net investment in plant rather than an expenditure, is now recognized as an expense decreasing unrestricted net assets because it involves a systematic measurement of the using up of plant assets. Another accounting change is that owed vacations and retiree nonpension benefits will have to be carried as liabilities. In general, in anticipating questions about the availability of unrestricted net assets, the notes to the financial statements will play a far greater role in clarifying the information. These notes could include self-imposed limitations (previously quasi endowments) and contractual limitations. However, only externally imposed restrictions will constitute permanently or temporarily restricted endowments. Otherwise, endowments must be classified as unrestricted.

Another requirement of SFAS No. 117 is a statement of activities, for which only general guidance is provided. Again, the donor-imposed restrictions play a major role. Without restrictions, revenues are reported as increases in unrestricted net assets and expenses are reported as decreases in unrestricted net assets.

Budget flexibility will be determined in part by the interaction between reserves held as assets (i.e., funds functioning as endowments) and reserves held as fund liabilities (e.g., owed vacations and retiree nonpension benefits). These choices are new and important and can lead to greater long-term flexibility if managed with short-term discipline.

GASB has a project underway to test alternative display models for financial statements for public institutions.

Hidden Costs that Limit Flexibility

Budgeters do not like to be surprised by unexpected expenditures. In designing budgets they usually include estimates for equipment and facilities repair and replacement, or they establish contingency funds to enable the institution to take advantage of opportunities or respond to emergencies. However, many policy decisions, such as those involving the addition of new facilities, the introduction of new degree programs, or the revision of curricula, carry with them hidden costs that become long-term obligations. Opening a new building, for example, will require funds for utilities and building maintenance. A new facility also usually needs an initial allocation for equipment and furnishings. If this allocation is significant, funds also will have to be provided for equipment maintenance.

The obvious costs of a new degree program are the salaries of additional faculty and staff and the operating expenses associated with day-to-day program administration. New programs also seem to arouse expectations for continued growth. Less obvious are the demands that the new program makes on existing programs. If the new program attracts new students to the institution, the demand for courses in existing programs that are complementary will increase. This may require additional instructors to be hired in those disciplines. If, on the other hand, the new program attracts students from other degree programs, there may be a decline in students taking courses in certain existing departments. Thus, the courses in some departments may become undersubscribed, leaving those departments relatively overstaffed.

Altering the curriculum of one department's program may have fiscal implications for other departments. If, for example, the accounting program changes its requirements to include instruction in computer science, the computer science department may have to employ additional faculty to meet the increased demand. Similarly, if a number of degree programs include a requirement for one or more accounting courses, the accounting department may have to add faculty. In the early 1980s, the University of Maryland, College Park, added a junior-level English composition requirement to all curricula. All students were required to take such a course to graduate. The fiscal implications of this curricular modification, which were not evaluated prior to campus senate approval of the measure, included the addition of classroom sections at an approximate cost of $250,000. This new cost required the reallocation of funds from other academic programs. One question raised by these examples is, "Who should provide the resources to meet the increased or shifted demand for instruction?" Clearly, more than one department must bear the burden of curricular changes that affect several programs. The question then is whether the new programs are worthwhile in view of the explicit and hidden costs.

The elimination of activities or programs may have hidden costs that erase some or all of the planned savings. For example, administrators of programs that require courses or services from the program being eliminated will have to find substitutes or provide the services themselves. If personnel are being released, the institution may be obligated to place them in other positions on campus or to provide some severance pay. Facilities that are being "mothballed" because of program curtailment may require security and services and minimal heating during the winter months.

Personnel decisions can have long-term costs if they involve positions protected by tenure or some form of job security. One cost is the loss of budget flexibility. Job permanence makes it difficult for budgeters to reallocate positions from one activity to another or to reduce the number of positions in an activity. Moreover, tenured positions require a significant financial investment. If one assumes that an assistant professor is tenured and promoted at age 30 and continues to serve until age 70 at a level salary of $50,000 throughout his or her career, the institution makes a $2 million commitment upon awarding tenure.

Hidden costs may also be a factor when new programs and activities are initiated with seed funding from endowments or grants. Once the program or activity is underway and the seed money has been consumed, it may be necessary to provide continued funding to keep the enterprise alive. There is a natural tendency to want to guarantee the success of initial investments by continuing to invest funds in the new programs and activities. If the long-term financial needs of a new enterprise are anticipated and sources of funding have been identified, there will be fewer hidden costs.

Strategies for Allocating Resources And Increasing Flexibility

The Regulated Environment: Constraints and Opportunities

Fiscal transactions in both public and independent institutions are governed by an array of accounting, personnel, and purchasing policies and procedures and federal regulations. Independent institutions have more control over their policies and procedures than do public institutions, which usually must conform to guidelines for all state agencies, but professional standards in accounting, personnel, and purchasing tend to be widely adopted and thereby limit any advantage the private sector might enjoy. In addition, collective bargaining agreements in both the public and private sectors affect budgeters' flexibility.

Accounting policies and procedures. The complex structure of accounts that many institutions have is intended to guarantee that funds can be monitored and spent only for intended purposes. For example, many institutions, especially public ones, are restricted in the use of their salaries and wages funds to personnel expenditures only. Operating expenses funds, however, can sometimes be used for salaries and wages as well as for day-to-day costs of operations, including communication, travel, office supplies, and equipment. Sometimes accounts established to pay for visiting lecturers' honoraria or contractual arrangements with individuals can be replenished by both salaries and wages funds and operating expenses funds. Often accounts are established to track certain kinds of income and to ensure that the revenues are spent for specified purposes. Accounts for student activity fees, laboratory fees, or instructional materials fees are examples of this category. For the same reason, accounts set up to receive research funds can be used only for project expenditures.

The degree to which faculty and staff adhere to accounting policies and procedures is determined by internal, state, and federal auditors. These auditors examine not only the accuracy of account statements but also the appropriateness of transfers and expenditures and the adequacy of the accounting framework.

The prospective budgeter needs to understand several aspects of the accounting structure. What is the range of expenditures that can be made from each account? To what extent can funds or charges be transferred across accounts? (Reserves in one part of the account structure may not be useful in other parts; similarly, flexibility in adjusting the accounts may be restricted.)

Personnel policies and procedures. Because salaries and wages account for most of an institution's budget, it seems reasonable to expect that a large part of a budgeter's flexibility will be controlled by institutional personnel policies and procedures. Contract and tenure obligations represent long-term financial commitments on the part of the institution. The manner in which faculty salary structures are set and the ease with which adjustments can be made strongly influence the institution's competitiveness in recruiting new faculty. Likewise, support staff salary structures, whether based on local market conditions, union pay scales, or statewide public employee scales, affect the ability to hire and retain good staff. If the institution must conform to a state employee salary scale, for example, it may not be able to attract individuals with the special skills required.

Contractual and tenure policies specify the lengths of probationary periods, the amount of advance notice to be given for termination of appointment, schedules for performance review, and grievance procedures. In some states these schedules are specified by law, and budget planning is clearly dependent on them. Moreover, the policies governing the appointment of temporary and part-time personnel will determine some of the boundaries of budget flexibility. Faculty research appointments that parallel tenure-track appointments may provide programs with staffing flexibility in that research appointments can be made without the usual tenure commitment.

Princeton University, for example, attempted to build flexibility into its staffing of degree programs by establishing a tenure quota, or a maximum ratio of tenured to total faculty on a department-by-department basis. Departments at the tenure ceiling could not make tenured appointments until a tenured faculty member departed. Exceptions to the departmental tenure quotas were made when excellent opportunities existed for faculty recruitment. Although the tenure quotas placed considerable pressure on junior nontenured faculty, the policy was clearly presented and well publicized so that junior faculty knew in advance the probabilities of attaining tenure.

Controlling the number of tenured faculty is only one concern in the application of tenure quotas. Another consideration is the age distribution of tenured faculty. If, for example, the ages are clustered, many faculty will have to be replaced at the same time, when the average retirement age is reached.

Tenure quotas can be used to control the number of tenure commitments in situations of declining enrollment. The disadvantages of quotas include limited opportunities for junior faculty, considerable pressure on those faculty, and the potential exclusion of superior faculty from tenure.

Purchasing policies and procedures. Procurement regulations are intended to facilitate the orderly and economical purchase of goods and services. As with any bureaucratic procedures, their weight and complexity alone often conspire to undermine convenience and limit flexibility. In many institutions, for example, all purchase requests are funneled through a purchasing department. The volume of activity through this support unit usually dictates how quickly the purchase can be made. Toward the end of the fiscal year, when most campus units are attempting to spend the balances in their operating expenses budgets, the volume of purchase requests is very high and the delays are more frequent. These delays in the purchasing department may in turn cause suspension of some activity in the requesting unit or the loss of early-payment discounts.

In many public institutions, the purchasing procedures are governed by state regulations. Ceilings are often specified above which purchase requests must be placed out on bid. In some cases the bid requests must be advertised (e.g., in the state register) for prescribed lengths of time before purchases can be made. Generally, the purchase must be made through the low bidder; exceptions must be justified to the appropriate authorities. Some states require that proposed purchases over a certain value be reviewed by a state agency before the purchase is actually made. In a growing number of states, certain classes of proposed purchases, especially those involving computer-related expenditures, must be reviewed by state agencies. These purchase regulations restrict the maneuverability of budgeters, particularly their flexibility to spend resources as they wish. Flexibility thus becomes a matter of timing as well as the identification of reserve resources.

Financial reporting. All institutions have financial reporting systems to control the flow of funds. Most of these systems have evolved over time. More current systems seek to satisfy not only the need to control expenditures, but also to provide information that can be used to manage resources. It is important for budgeters to understand the limitations of their own institution's accounting and budget systems. A knowledge of where data come from is a first step to understanding how the data can be used and how they are inherently limited. Budgeters' expectations for management of information may not be met if the financial reporting system has only a control orientation. Even financial reporting systems that support resource management offer data that suggest questions rather than definitive answers about the institution.

Federal regulations. In seeking to ensure that federal funds are used only for the purpose for which they were granted, the federal government has burdened colleges and universities with a complex set of regulations that absorb considerable institutional time and money. Although these regulations are well intentioned, their implementation has severely strained the flexibility of administrators and faculty in day-to-day operations.

The federal government requires, for example, a strict accounting of the use of contract and grant funds and the costs assessed by institutions as indirect cost reimbursement charges. Accounting for indirect costs alone is a time-consuming and inexact science at best. Tracking faculty and staff time is even more difficult. Faculty members involved simultaneously in more than one sponsored research activity must account for their time commitment to each project. This distribution of time must then be translated by the controller's office into differential charges against the various research accounts. Most college and university payroll systems have difficulty responding to the fluctuating commitments to multiple sponsored activities, so typically the charges on a monthly or semester basis are averaged as dictated by the faculty member's cumulative distribution of time to the various projects.

Record keeping is perhaps even more troublesome for support staff. A secretary, for example, may be responsible to five or six faculty members, each of whom has externally supported research in addition to his or her teaching and service commitments. It is almost impossible to monitor the secretary's effort accurately in terms of commitment to specific research projects, teaching obligations, and professional activities. It is not uncommon for the federal government to accuse institutions of using research funds to support instructional and other activities.

Many of these problems arise from the difficulties in separating and monitoring commitments to multiple activities. In some cases, such as the support of graduate students or postdoctoral fellows, research training is a part of research activity and is acceptable to the federal government. Increased federal oversight in recent years, especially through Office of Management and Budget Circular A-21 regulations, and as evidenced by the infamous case of Stanford University in the early 1990s, has encouraged colleges and universities to improve and expand their accounting systems.

Despite restrictions associated with the use of federal funds, some flexibility is nonetheless permitted. Faculty and staff travel supported by contracts and grants may release institutional funds that otherwise would have been earmarked for travel. Some contracts and grants support the purchase of expensive equipment that can be used for graduate student training as well as research. Contracts and grants often support graduate students as research assistants, thereby increasing the availability of financial assistance to the institution. Furthermore, some grants and contracts provide salary funds to allow faculty to support staff and purchase release time from the institution for their own activities. The salary money saved in this manner can be used to hire part-time faculty to meet instructional commitments or additional support staff. In some institutions the budgeting systems are such that funds equivalent to a portion of the indirect cost reimbursements might be used by the institution to provide seed funding for new or junior faculty or to encourage departments to undertake new research.

Collective bargaining. The existence of a collective bargaining agreement at an institution will restrict the actions that may be taken by the administration during the budget process. Collective bargaining agreements almost always contain stipulated salary increases, rates of pay for summer school and overtime, and mandated employee benefits. These contractual agreements may be modified only with the assent of the collective bargaining representative. Normally, previously negotiated compensation increases are not reduced by a collective bargaining representative, except, on occasion, to prevent layoffs. Because some collective bargaining agreements extend over three or four years, accurate long-range projections of salary expenses are crucial for determining affordable compensation levels.

Although most collective bargaining agreements state specific future salary increases, some agreements have made these increases, or parts thereof, conditional on such factors as inflation, student enrollment, and state appropriations.

In addition, most collective bargaining agreements specify the workload of the faculty. Thus, the institution may not unilaterally increase this workload during the term of the agreement in response to unexpected revenue shortfalls. Furthermore, some agreements restrict the use of part-time faculty as replacements for full-time faculty. Union approval may also need to be sought for early-retirement programs for tenured faculty.

The collective bargaining agreement will almost certainly specify retrenchment procedures, including the order of retrenchment, the required due notice or severance salary, and the required consultation that must precede the retrenchment of faculty. Any plan to resolve a budget crisis through retrenchment must take into account these restrictions and the cost of terminating personnel. For example, some institutions are self-insured for unemployment compensation (i.e., the institution must reimburse the state for payments made to any employee laid off).

Some agreements contain other restrictions with indirect budget implications. The agreement may forbid the use of tenure quotas. In addition, incentives to seek outside funding may be included. For example, the Temple University collective bargaining agreement returns to the dean of each college 10 percent of the increase in overhead recovery on grants. This provides a financial incentive for the dean and faculty of each college to seek additional outside grant support. However, the overhead funds given to the dean and faculty are also available to the central administration.

Collective agreements allow precise determination of personnel costs well in advance, though they hinder the ability to reduce these costs when unexpected financial problems occur.

Public Institutions

The regulated environment of public institutions extends beyond those areas mentioned above to include restrictions concerning state appropriations to institutions (see figure 4.3).

Formula allocation procedures. Generally, budget formulas are used as a means to generate institutional requests for funds. By their very nature, formulas are simplified models of the complex expenditure patterns of institutions. A danger in the use of formulas is that decision makers far removed from institutional operations may rely on formulas for an understanding of how the institution actually functions. If, for example, decision makers believe that faculty in some disciplines are not teaching enough students and propose that student-faculty ratios be increased, the net budget effect at the institution might not be what was planned. Although adjusting the formula to a higher student-faculty ratio might reduce resources, campus decision makers might decide to absorb the reduction by assigning graduate students heavier teaching loads rather than increasing the burden on faculty. Similarly, decision makers may lighten the impact of a reduction in faculty travel funds by an internal transfer of funds from supplies or equipment to the travel account.

Figure 4.3 Regulation of Public Institutions

Public institutions can be additionally regulated in the following ways:

- ☐ Through allocation procedures
- ☐ Through enrollment ceilings
- ☐ Through appropriations bill language
- ☐ Through funding ceilings
- ☐ Through position control
- ☐ Through restrictions on the use of year-end balances
- ☐ Through line-item budget reductions
- ☐ Through salary savings targets

The restrictiveness of formula allocation procedures stems not from their use as a means to generate budget requests, but from the perception of formulas as an implicit or explicit commitment of how funds will be utilized. The more that state-level decision makers perceive the formula as an instrument of accountability, the more complex the formula will have to become to mirror the richness of institutional activity and the more restrictive the budget environment becomes.

Enrollment ceilings. To limit institutional demands on the state treasury, some states have placed enrollment ceilings on institutions. In imposing ceilings, states generally agree to support instructional and other costs up to the target enrollments, but require the institution to absorb the costs of educating students in excess of the ceiling. Enrollment ceilings have also been used by state-level policy makers as a mechanism to redistribute enrollments among public institutions within a state. Ceilings are imposed on institutions with the highest student demand, thereby, in theory, discouraging excess enrollments and encouraging students to seek admission to underenrolled institutions. The net effect on the institution that has enrollment ceilings is a limiting of state appropriations.

Some states apply the concept of enrollment thresholds in making their appropriations to institutions. The state establishes a bandwidth for enrollment projections of, for example, plus or minus 2 percent. If actual enrollments fall within that range, the appropriation is unchanged. If enrollments exceed the projection by more than the bandwidth, the state will provide funds for the additional enrollments (usually those over the bandwidth). Similarly, if enrollments are lower than the projection by more than the bandwidth, the institution must return funds. In this example, the institution is responsible for the enrollments if they exceed projections by up to 2 percent; it gains excess funds if the actual enrollments are up to 2 percent less than projected.

Appropriations bill language. The contents of the appropriations bill determine much of a public institution's flexibility. Some states do not appropriate funds that are received directly by the institution: tuition income, student and other fees, contract and grant funding. Other states have detailed appropriations that include all of the above items. In states with detailed appropriations, intense negotiations frequently occur between institutions and state officials concerning estimates of these kinds of income. State officials tend to estimate liberally; institutional officials tend to estimate conservatively. In general, the fewer the items included in the appropriations bill, the more control the institution has over that income.

Often the appropriations bill contains language indicating legislative intent. This portion of the bill may address such topics as faculty productivity, student-faculty ratios, travel, campus security, and computer facilities and operations. In California, for example, the legislature's joint appropriations committee once inserted language in the appropriations bill calling for the elimination of $75,000 from the budget of the University of California, Berkeley, because the degree program in demography had allegedly been dropped. (The irony of the situation was that the legislator introducing the control language mistakenly read demography as dermatology, which was not a program on the Berkeley campus.) Although the control language is separate from the actual appropriations, the connection between the two is explicit and generally must be heeded if the institution does not wish to suffer a financial penalty at the hands of an irate legislature.

State agency staff control. Control over public institutions is exerted not only through state regulations and the language of appropriations bills, but also informally through the actions of the various state agency staffs. Higher education coordinating and governing board staffs are heavily involved in the drafting of statewide plans for higher education, reviewing new and existing degree programs, collecting data, establishing enrollment ceilings, reviewing budget requests, and reviewing plans for capital expenditures. Legislative fiscal staffs and executive budget office staffs shape and interpret policy in the same way they review higher education budget requests and control higher education expenditures once funds have been appropriated. Often the informal development of policy by these state agency staffs is not subject to tight control by the state's elected officials.

Position control. In some states the appropriations bill specifies not only the dollar amounts available to public institutions, but also the number of faculty and staff positions that can be filled. Clearly, position control limits the way in which salaries and wages funds are expended and limits the flexibility of institutional decision makers to staff their operations as needed. State-level policy makers frequently mention two reasons for the importance of position control. It establishes a ceiling on employment in the public sector in the state that affords politicians the chance to convince taxpayers that state government is under control. In addition, some state governments assume responsibility for benefits packages by way of central accounts (rather than including benefits packages in appropriations to state agencies). Under this arrangement policy makers need to be able to project the size of the benefits package that has to be set aside for the central account. This projection becomes much more difficult if there is no control over the number of staff positions.

How institutions minimize the impact of state position control depends in large part on personnel policies. In some personnel structures, temporary appointments of six months or less are not counted against an institution's position total. Moreover, it may be possible to reappoint temporary faculty or staff without a break in service and not have the appointment charged against the institution's position total. Some campuses establish pools of vacant positions and allocate these to various units. If, for example, a campus has 1,000 faculty and staff positions authorized by the state, of which 50 are vacant at any particular time, campus units might be permitted to fill 50 more positions than currently allocated. Because vacancies might not appear in units where additional staff are most needed, the pool vacancies can be reallocated on a year-to-year basis.

Year-end balances. In many states the balances remaining in state agency accounts at the end of the fiscal year revert to the state treasury. Unless otherwise controlled, most institutions spend a considerable portion of their budgets in the last several months of the fiscal year in an effort to expend all of their available resources. Given current incentives, this behavior is rational—a common assumption is that an organization or agency that cannot spend all of its appropriation within the fiscal year should have its budget reduced the following year. Incentives must be altered so that the rational person will do what is desirable, namely, spend resources only for what is necessary.

Some states employ fiscal controls instead of positive incentives to discourage uneven spending patterns. They control the rate of institutional expenditures through the allotment process, whereby funds appropriated to institutions are released by the state treasury on an installment basis (e.g., annually, quarterly, monthly). The more frequent the allotments, generally, the less control the institution has over the timing of its expenditures. (That is, the institution may not be able to commit funds until it has actually received them from the state treasury.)

Some states have adopted a carry-over policy for a part or all of state agency year-end balances. As a positive incentive for good fiscal management, state agencies are allowed to retain some or all of their account balances from one fiscal year to another. This policy discourages hurried and unplanned year-end spending. It also permits institutions to save enough funds from one fiscal year to another to make expensive purchases that could not otherwise be made within one fiscal year. Implicit in this policy is that prudent budgeters will always have some positive balance in their accounts as a hedge against the uncertainty of price changes, the delays in reporting that occur in most accounting systems, and unanticipated expenses. Many budgeters purposely wait to make major expenditures until late in the budget cycle to ensure that resources are available for emergencies. This category of year-end spending is carefully planned and not hurried. To require that all year-end balances revert to the state treasury is to penalize the careful money manager. Even in states in which year-end balances do revert to the treasury, most institutions have some accounts that automatically carry over balances from one fiscal year to another. These accounts, often called carry-over or revolving accounts, are typically designated for special purposes, including sponsored research and auxiliary enterprises. Transfers between these revolving accounts and the usual state accounts generally are regulated tightly to prevent the abuse of revolving accounts as "laundries" for carrying state funds across fiscal years.

Salary savings targets. A number of states have introduced a management device known as salary savings, budgetary savings, turnover savings, or forced savings. State agencies are targeted to return a percentage of their budgets (usually a percentage of the salaries and wages budget only) to the state treasury prior to the end of the fiscal year. These targets typically range from 1 to 4 percent of the salaries and wages budget. Thus, if an institution receives an appropriation of $10 million in salaries and wages and is assigned a 4 percent salary savings target, it may spend only $9.6 million in salaries and wages and must return $0.4 million to the state treasury.

The practice of salary savings evolved from the historical pattern of year-end savings that accrue to most organizations because of personnel attrition and the usual delays experienced in refilling positions. State-level policy makers observed that these savings in appropriated salaries and wages ranged from 2 to 4 percent. Rather than wait until the end of the fiscal year to collect whatever salary money went unspent, policy makers decided to set salary savings targets in advance to guarantee a known return. In this way the targeted savings could be allocated in advance (i.e., prior to the beginning of the fiscal year), thereby expanding the base of available state resources. Although most targets were based originally on historical patterns of natural salary savings, most states have adjusted the targets to reflect the need for additional resources and the perceived availability of those resources within state agencies. In some states, the method for setting salary savings targets is not very sophisticated: if state agencies complain loudly about the targets, state budget officials know that too much has been demanded. Some states also use an increase in the salary savings target to fund a portion of legislatively mandated salary increases. If, for example, a legislature appropriates a 5 percent salary increase, it may provide public institutions with funds sufficient for a 4.25 percent increase. The balance of the increase, 0.75 percent, must be provided internally through an increased salary savings target.

Typically, campus-level administrators distribute the campus target to all units supported by state funds. This distribution is often made on the basis of pro-rata shares of the campus salaries and wages budget, although adjustments might be made to reflect economies of scale of larger units (i.e., larger units generally have more personnel turnover in absolute terms than smaller units and therefore are in a better position to absorb a larger share of the salary savings target than their proportion of the campus salaries and wages budget would otherwise dictate). Any administrative layers between the campus administration and the department or activity are allocated a target and distribute it in turn to the units under their responsibility. The imposition of salary savings targets requires that the careful department chairperson or administrator identify in advance the source of the savings. This advance planning is all the more important in that position vacancies occur unevenly across campuses. Sometimes staff positions must be held vacant simply to allow sufficient savings to accumulate to meet the target obligation. Sponsored research funding that provides faculty release time, sabbatical leaves, and leaves of absence without pay becomes a source of salary savings for academic departments. Because the first obligation to be met with "flexible" salary money is salary savings, the savings target ultimately limits the fiscal flexibility of all units across the campus.

Institutions in the public sector have much less control over the budget process once the budget request leaves the institution. The process itself, for example, cannot be modified unless the state-level actors take action. Institutional actors can raise questions about several significant policy issues, but their success in changing state-level policy direction depends in large part on the persuasiveness of the arguments, the fiscal implications of changes as seen from the state perspective, and the receptivity to such arguments on the part of key state-level decision makers.

Relationship between state policy makers and higher education institutions. At the state level, most important decision makers view policy issues through their staffs. Thus, the governor depends heavily on his or her executive budget office to collect and analyze data and to make recommendations concerning the details of the budget. Similarly, legislators depend on staff members of the legislative fiscal staff(s) for much of their understanding of budgets. On rare occasions, however, these key actors examine higher education without the filtering effect of the staff. The governor may meet formally with the presidents of institutions or informally with faculty and institutional staff members who are personal friends. Legislators may also have informal relationships with faculty and staff. More commonly, legislators examine higher education directly through budget hearings. Staffs of state higher education coordinating and governing boards generally have the most frequent contact with institutions, although this contact tends to be through administrators.

Because of the relative infrequency of such contacts, their importance cannot be overemphasized. Institutional representatives, whether acting formally or informally, are under considerable pressure to represent the whole institution when they speak. Sometimes there is the temptation to risk the entire institutional budget for the sake of a special interest in one small part of the budget. Although only a small part is argued or defended in a hearing or meeting, the full budget is under the scrutiny of state-level decision makers. Accordingly, institutional representatives are usually careful to place their commentary in an appropriate context. State-level actors are extremely busy and seek information about state programs from every possible source. If handled sensitively, the face-to-face contact between institutional and state-level representatives can be an opportunity for selling budgets and programs.

Contact between state-level staff and institutional representatives occurs frequently outside the context of budget hearings. Many of the perceptions of higher education formed by state-level staff members are based on these encounters. The same cautions that apply when institutional actors engage key state-level decision makers also apply to any dealings with the staffs of those state-level persons. In particular, lobbying activities should be coordinated to be effective.

Issues that might be discussed by institutional and state-level budgeters vary in nature and importance from one state to another. The following list is illustrative rather than exhaustive.

> **Budget formulas.** Funding levels for many public institutions are determined by budget formulas. Such formulas in the instructional area are for the most part driven by student enrollments. Many formulas distinguish between graduate and undergraduate instruction; some distinguish among levels of instruction by degree program, academic department, or form of instruction (such as primarily lecture, mixture of lecture and small-group discussion, and laboratory). Many discussions concerning formulas focus on the philosophical underpinnings or on the technical aspects of the formula: Should formulas be enrollment driven? How should enrollment-driven formulas be modified for situations of enrollment decline? Can funding mechanisms be developed that function on the basis of marginal costs? What should be the relative formula weights among degree programs, among levels of instruction, and among forms of instruction?

> **State appropriations.** How does the state determine its equitable share of the costs of public instruction? How does the state determine an equitable distribution of resources among institutions? What is the relationship between state policy on faculty workload and state appropriations?

Auxiliary enterprises. What are the state's policies concerning support of auxiliary enterprises? Should the state have as much control as it does over auxiliary activities? Can institutional autonomy be increased while state needs for accountability are met?

Continuing education/evening programs/summer programs. To what extent should the state fund continuing education, evening programs, and summer programs? Should these be self-supporting? Can institutions market and advertise for such programs? To what extent will the continuing education program at one institution compete with the instructional programs at other institutions?

Budget reviews. At what level of detail should budgets be reviewed by state officials? How much information about the operation of institutions should be provided? At what level of detail in a budget review does the autonomy of institutions begin to erode?

Tuition levels. How much control should state officials have in establishing tuition levels? What portion of the costs of higher education should be borne by the student through tuition charges? Do state financial aid policies take tuition policies into account? Should there be different tuition charges for different degree programs and different student levels?

Enrollment ceilings. Some states have set enrollment ceilings for each institution as a means of limiting higher education budgets. Should enrollment ceilings be used to redirect students from certain institutions to others?

Financial crisis. How should the higher education community and the state establish processes to develop and review institutional plans for program reductions and mission changes as enrollments decline? What will happen to higher education in the face of falling state revenues or tax and expenditure limitations that force reductions in funding regardless of enrollment trends?

Institutional Strategies to Increase Flexibility

A number of specific strategies can be adopted to increase flexibility.

Changing the framework. Although it would be difficult to quantify, a considerable amount of flexibility in most institutions has been eroded or has disappeared over time because the framework for budgeting within the institution has not been reexamined regularly. Given the press of time during the budget cycle, the natural tendency of budgeters is to allocate resources largely on the basis of history (i.e., the previous year's budget). Patterns of allocation are adjusted marginally either across the board or in response to special requests made by individual units. The inertia of history is recognizable in the asymmetry of program growth and program decline. When a unit's activities expand, the unit typically requests increases in personnel and operating expenses to accommodate the increased workload. When the unit's activities decline, however, there usually is not an equally rigorous mechanism to ensure that the expenses of running the unit are reviewed and, if possible, reduced.

An institution may be able to recover slack resources by carefully analyzing the distribution of resources across the campus. The best approach seems to be an analysis of portions of the budget at any one time, or an analysis of how portions of the budget relate to one another (e.g., academic affairs and administrative support and student affairs). Zero-base budgeting or its variants, which construct the costs of all programs and activities by examining the costs of all program elements (see appendix), or some form of degree and service program analysis might be applied to closely related academic or support programs. Another analytical strategy might be to investigate activities across common dimensions, such as secretarial or support staffing, operating expenses budgets, the use of graduate assistants in academic departments, or faculty/staff workloads.

An analytical approach that has gained some currency in both inter- and intrainstitutional studies is the examination of fixed and variable costs. Fixed costs represent the base expenditure for the operation of an institution or activity below which operations could not occur. In essence, fixed costs represent the thresholds for activities. A liberal arts curriculum, for example, requires some core of faculty representing certain disciplines (e.g., philosophy, English, history, art) to be considered a curriculum, and an institution requires a certain minimum of facilities or space. This core is supplemented to reflect increases in workload or improvements in the quality of activities. Unless the pattern of resource allocation is periodically studied in detail, the core of fixed costs for most activities or institutions increases with time. If one embraces the principle that fewer fixed costs mean more flexibility, the objective of the budgeter becomes obvious: to "unfix" the fixed costs. In other words, the assumption that some costs are fixed should be challenged regularly during budget reviews. Experienced budgeters have observed that when program and activity planning are linked in advance to the budget process, costs become more variable.

Central reserve. Perhaps the most obvious strategy is to create a central reserve of resources (at the institution, college, or department level) by withholding a small percentage of the funds to be distributed to lower levels in the institution. If, for example, an institution projects an increase in revenue of 10 percent for the coming fiscal year, the president may elect to withhold one-tenth of the amount (or 1 percent of the institutional budget) in a discretionary fund. Similarly, deans may elect to withhold a small percentage of increases in revenue from their colleges or schools and use this pool of resources for discretionary purposes. In turn, the department chairperson may decide to hold back a small part of the faculty and staff salary increment pool as a departmental reserve.

Although some central reserve is essential as a buffer against the uncertainty of a year's budget, the degree to which persons at lower levels in the institutional hierarchy become dependent on this surplus pool determines how much flexibility the reserve truly offers. If departments in a college regularly petition the dean for supplementary support from the dean's contingency fund, and if the dean regularly provides some or all of the resources requested, the contingency fund becomes de facto a part of the college's regular budget. The contingency fund remains a flexible resource only if it is used for emergencies or unusual opportunities. Central reserves should be viewed as a short-term safety net to keep useful activities going until alternative permanent funding sources are identified. The reserves themselves should not be seen as a permanent source of support for the activities.

Salary or budget savings. In both independent and public institutions reserves can be established through the imposition of a salary or budget savings target on units lower in the institutional hierarchy. Budgeters in public institutions are usually obligated to meet a state-imposed target; accordingly, campus-level officials increase the targets of subordinate units to exceed the state obligation and thereby create a small reserve. If, for example, the state targets a small public college for $500,000 in salary savings, the president or chief budget officer may allocate salary savings targets of $600,000 to create a central reserve of $100,000 for the president. Budgeters in the campus-level administrations of independent institutions can either set institutionwide salary or budget savings targets based on historical natural savings balances or target programs and activities to conform to institutional objectives.

Within institutions that employ salary or budget savings targets, budgeters at every level of the hierarchy have a natural tendency to set higher targets for subordinate units so as to provide a cushion of reserves. This setting of targets for subordinate units is a means of shifting uncertainty to other levels of the authority hierarchy.

Formula adjustments. In some state systems that employ budget formulas, institutions may be able to adjust the formula parameters to their advantage. Although such strategies to gain flexibility generally are not encouraged, they illustrate how budgeters take advantage of the underlying incentive structures of the formulas. In situations where the budget formulas are based on the number of student credit hours taught per faculty member, some institutions have increased the credit hour value of certain courses (e.g., physical education, which is taken by many students) to increase artificially the student credit hour productivity of the institution. Formulas that differentiate by level of instruction for credit hour productivity (i.e., credit hours in graduate-level courses are weighted more than credit hours in upper-division courses, which in turn are weighted more than credit hours in lower-division courses) have encouraged some institutions to raise the level of certain courses (e.g., to shift courses from the lower division to the upper division) to gain additional funding. In those states that use enrollment-driven formulas but do not assess penalties for enrolling below projections (the penalty would be the reversion of excess funds to the state), some institutions make optimistic enrollment projections, especially at the higher student levels (e.g., graduate or upper division) that have more weight in the funding formula. State agencies frequently audit the data used in formulas to discourage such improper activities.

Position reversion. Institutions can gain some flexibility through a policy of requiring that all vacant faculty and staff positions in subordinate units revert to the control of a dean or central administrator for possible reallocation.

Reduction of the grade or rank of vacant positions. Some slack resources can be gained by downgrading the grade or rank of a position when it becomes vacant and shifting the salary savings to other areas. For example, if a full professor earning $65,000 per year departs, the department chairperson might wish to fill the vacancy with an assistant professor earning $35,000 annually. The difference of $30,000 can be diverted to other salaries and wages. As a variant of the position reversion strategy, administrators might automatically downgrade the grade or rank of vacant positions in units under their purview and retain the salary savings. This strategy must be used selectively, however, so as not to undermine the integrity of the program or activity. An academic department, for example, requires a core of senior faculty to provide leadership. Similarly, an academic or administrative support unit may not be able to function well with underexperienced support staff.

Employment of part-time or temporary faculty. A common source of flexibility is the employment of part-time or temporary faculty in place of permanent faculty. Temporary faculty employed on a course-by-course basis generally are much less expensive than tenured faculty. Some department chairpersons purposely hold certain faculty lines vacant so that the funds can be used to employ temporary faculty, thereby increasing the department's teaching capacity. Departments often employ part-time or temporary faculty to replace permanent faculty who are on sabbatical leave or leave of absence without pay. The salary savings can be used for student labor, graduate or research assistants, or additional secretarial support, or for salary savings targets imposed by higher levels of authority.

Institutions that depend heavily on temporary faculty must carefully weigh the advantages and drawbacks. Temporary faculty often become academic nomads, moving from one temporary position to another each semester or year because they are unable to find permanent positions in a tight job market. Temporary faculty are frequently not as available to students and colleagues as are permanent faculty. In the public sector, state-level policy makers who observe that institutions keep faculty positions vacant in order to employ temporary faculty may decide to reduce the number of permanent faculty positions allocated to those institutions.

Withholding of some salary adjustment funds. In public systems, the legislature often appropriates funds for salary adjustments based on the number of authorized faculty and staff lines and the current salaries on those lines. To create a central reserve, campus-level administrators might allocate salary adjustment funds to subordinate units only for those lines currently filled. The salary adjustment funds provided by the state for vacant lines would be retained by campus-level administrators as slack resources. Some of these resources might be used, for example, to increase the salaries of faculty or staff who have been promoted as of the new fiscal year.

Revolving funds. In most state systems, fund balances remaining at the end of the fiscal year revert to the state treasury. Similarly, in many independent institutions, year-end balances revert to the president or chief executive officer for use as a reserve or as part of the following year's budget. Most campuses have activities such as sponsored research or auxiliary enterprises with budgets that continue across fiscal years, primarily because the funds involved are not provided by the state. Sometimes these budgets, in the form of revolving or carry-over accounts, can be used to carry regular institutional funds across fiscal years. At the end of the fiscal year it may be possible, for example, to transfer charges that have accumulated during the year against the revolving fund to accounts consisting of regular institutional funds. Federal reporting and accounting regulations have made it difficult to effect such transfers with federally sponsored program accounts, although these transfers generally are permissible in other revolving accounts.

Balance carryovers. State systems or independent institutions that permit the carry over of year-end balances from one fiscal year to another (whereby a part or all of the balances may be retained) have a natural source of budget flexibility. This liberal use of year-end balances reduces the pressure on units to spend all of their resources at year's end and encourages the saving of resources for major purchases or projects.

Sponsored programs. Sponsored research and training activities supported by external funding sources provide institutions with the opportunity for considerable flexibility. Grant and contract proposals include many direct costs (e.g., secretarial support, graduate student support, travel, supplies and materials) that enhance the financial position of the institution. They also provide financial relief for research activities supported by the institution, but that legitimately can be supported externally.

Overhead reimbursement. Indirect costs charged to sponsored activities are computed on the basis of the actual expenses incurred by the institution in conducting the activities. To encourage sponsored research and training, some states allow institutions to use a portion of indirect cost reimbursement funds for discretionary purposes rather than requiring that the funds be used to offset the operating expenses incurred. In essence, these states are assuming part of the cost of the sponsored activities. Frequently, the overhead reimbursement funds retained by the institution are used as seed funding to encourage additional sponsored activities. (Such funds can provide, for example, faculty release time for proposal writing or equipment purchases or the establishment of laboratories for new or junior faculty.)

Research foundations and research institutes. Many state institutions with significant sponsored program activity establish private research foundations and institutes for receipt of certain grants, contracts, and gifts. Funds processed by these private foundations do not come under the scrutiny of state-level officials, and activities supported through these foundations are not subject to the usual state policies and procedures. If, for example, a state agency must review purchases that are in excess of some fixed amount, scrutiny can be avoided if the purchase is made with foundation funds. The flexibility obtained by creating a private research foundation or institute is defined by the organization's legal structure.

Sabbatical leave policy. Many institutions provide faculty members with sabbatical leaves for a full year at half-salary or for one-half year at full salary after the individual has served a specified time at the institution. To gain flexibility when resources are tight, some institutions have altered the standard policy to permit only sabbatical leaves for a full year at half-salary. This modification guarantees that the institution will have one-half of the faculty member's salary to use for temporary replacements or for other purposes.

For Further Reading

Strategic planning for the academic enterprise should dictate the allocation of resources. Accordingly, the literature on strategic planning in colleges and universities is essential reading for understanding the framework for directing resources toward high-priority activities. One of the best books on the subject is George Keller's *Academic Strategy: The Management Revolution in American Higher Education* (Baltimore: The Johns Hopkins University Press, 1983). An interesting counterpoint that discusses some of the difficulties of employing strategic planning is Frank A. Schmidtlein and Toby H. Milton, "College and University Planning: Perspectives from a Nation-Wide Study," *Planning for Higher Education 17, no. 3* (1988–89): 1–19.

The faculty role in strategic planning is analyzed by Susy S. Chan, "Faculty Participation in Strategic Planning: Incentives and Strategies," *Planning for Higher Education 16, no. 2* (1987–88): 19–30. See also Rebecca Stafford, "Sheep in Wolves' Clothing, or How Not to Do Strategic Planning," *Planning for Higher Education 22, no. 1* (Fall 1993): 55–59, a review of the strengths and weaknesses of many institutional strategic plans. Other overviews of strategic planning include Robert G. Cope, *Opportunity from Strength: Strategic Planning Clarified with Case Examples*, ASHE-ERIC Higher Education Report no. 8 (Washington, DC: Association for the Study of Higher Education, 1987); Douglas W. Steeples, Ed., *Successful Strategic Planning: Case Studies*, New Directions for Higher Education no. 64 (San Francisco: Jossey-Bass, Inc., 1988); and Frank A. Schmidtlein and Toby H. Milton, *Adapting Strategic Planning to Campus Realities*, New Directions for Institutional Research no. 67 (San Francisco: Jossey-Bass, Inc., 1990). An article still relevant more than a decade after it was published is Frederick E. Balderston, "Strategic Management Approaches for the 1980s: Navigating in the Trough," in Joseph Froomkin, ed., *The Crisis in Higher Education*, an issue of *Proceedings of the Academy of Political Science 35, no. 2* (1983).

The difficulties in relating planning and budgeting are discussed in several articles in a special issue of *Planning for Higher Education 18, no. 2* (1989-90): Richard J. Meisinger, Jr., "Introduction to Special Issues on the Relationship Between Planning and Budgeting"; Frank A. Schmidtlein, "Why Linking Budgets to Plans Has Proven Difficult in Higher Education"; Edward Foster, "Planning at the University of Minnesota"; and William F. Massy, "Budget Decentralization at Stanford University."

Improving the process of resource allocation is the objective of the monograph by David J. Berg and Gerald M. Skogley, eds., *Making the Budget Process Work*, New Directions for Higher Education no. 52 (San Francisco: Jossey-Bass, Inc., 1985). William Vandement has the same objective in *Managing Money in Higher Education: A Guide to the Financial Process and Effective Participation Within It* (San Francisco: Jossey-Bass, Inc., 1989). A primer on financial management is James A. Hyatt and Aurora A. Santiago, *Financial Management of Colleges and Universities* (Washington, DC: National Association of College and University Business Officers, 1986). An effort to rationalize the budget process is found in Ellen Earle Chaffee, *Rational Decisionmaking in Higher Education* (Boulder, CO: National Center for Higher Education Management Systems, 1983). The allocation of resources as seen through the conceptual lens of productivity is discussed in Richard E. Anderson and Joel W. Meyerson, eds., *Productivity & Higher Education: Improving the Effectiveness of Faculty, Facilities, and Financial Resources* (Princeton, NJ: Peterson's Guides, 1992). A companion volume is William F. Massy and Joel W. Meyerson, eds., *Strategy & Finance in Higher Education: Surviving the '90s* (Princeton, NJ: Peterson's Guides, 1992).

More and more attention is being given to the issues of cost and performance. On the subject of cost containment, see John S. Waggaman, *Strategies and Consequences: Managing the Costs in Higher Education*, ASHE-ERIC Higher Education Report no. 8 (Washington, DC: The George Washington University, 1991). Measuring performance is the subject of William F. Massy and Joel W. Meyerson, eds., *Measuring Institutional Performance in Higher Education* (Princeton, NJ: Peterson's Guides, 1994) and Barbara E. Taylor, Joel W. Meyerson, and William F. Massy, eds., *Strategic Indicators for Higher Education: Improving Performance* (Princeton, NJ: Peterson's Guides, 1993).

Several specialized volumes that address financial management issues include *Capital Formation Alternatives in Higher Education* (Washington, DC: National Association of College and University Business Officers, 1988); Robert T. Forrester, *A Handbook on Debt Management for Colleges and Universities* (Washington, DC: National Association of College and University Business Officers, 1988); and *Planning for Improved Campus Facilities* (Alexandria, VA: The Association of Higher Education Facilities Officers, 1992).

Notes

1. Burton Clark, *The Distinctive College: Antioch, Reed & Swarthmore* (Chicago: Aldine Publishing Company, 1970).
2. Paul Strohm, Indiana University, personal communication with the author, 1984.
3. National Association of College and University Business Officers, *NACUBO Endowment Study* (Washington: NACUBO, 1994).

FIVE
Retrenchment and Reallocation: Fiscal Issues

R etrenchment and reallocation embrace an array of actions that in the past were simply responses to fiscal crises, usually situations in which institutions had insufficient funds to maintain their current assortment of programs and activities. With the changing social, economic, and political environment of the 1990s, however, retrenchment and reallocation have become embedded in the operations of most colleges and universities. Higher education no longer enjoys the broad social support it had in the 1960s and 1970s. The costs of higher education have escalated faster than the consumer price index, forcing colleges and universities to make difficult choices. Moreover, the economic prospects for higher education show no signs of improvement over the next decade. As a result, strategies for retrenchment and reallocation will have to become a fixed part of the fabric of institutional decision making.

Retrenchment and reallocation tend to be viewed as negative actions, no doubt because of the unpleasantness accompanying these processes during the past several decades. Retrenchment, which involves the diminution of programs and activities because of a decline in resources, and reallocation, which involves shifting resources to reflect changing program priorities, affect an institution's employees. With up to 80 percent of some institutional budgets committed to salaries and benefits, it is difficult to find other parts of the budget that can be tapped for the often significant adjustments that have to be made. Ill-considered decisions that affect large numbers of people, be they faculty or staff, can haunt institutions for years and undermine their well-being. For example, the 1976 retrenchment at the City University of New York

153

(CUNY) is viewed in retrospect by faculty and administrators alike as having had disastrous consequences for morale. In addition, through the large-scale release of junior faculty, CUNY instantly shifted the demographic profile of faculty age significantly upwards. For any institution suddenly thrust into a financial crisis, the experience can be damaging. The purpose of this chapter is to encourage administrators and faculty to anticipate the new economic realities and to plan ways to avoid or at least minimize the effects.

Situations that call for retrenchment or reallocation should also be viewed as opportunities to effect changes that might not otherwise be implemented. During periods of growth, it is natural to avoid difficult decisions about programs that are lower priority. With sufficient resources it is possible to fund the expansion of higher-priority programs while continuing to support those of lesser importance. Lean times change the equation. If the transition to a reduced or realigned funding base can be managed with minimal loss of faculty and staff, the institution can emerge stronger and with improved morale.

Planning for Retrenchment and Reallocation

Many cases of financial stringency have caught institutions unprepared. Generally, the less time faculty and administrators have to react to a fiscal emergency, the narrower the range of options open to them. Moreover, with personnel salaries and benefits making up the largest part of institutional budgets, substantial reductions or shifts in resources often involve reduction in faculty and staff positions. These reductions are the most difficult to make and potentially have the greatest effect on institutional operations. The sooner faculty and administrators plan cooperatively for or anticipate financial problems, the more the institution can rely upon normal attrition and provide for informed faculty involvement.

Some of the worst aspects of financial retrenchment can be minimized through what Paul Strohm calls "pre-exigency planning."[1] Some students of organizational behavior argue that faculty and administrators are so entrenched in their routines and hold so firmly to their expectations that they need the spur of financial stress to motivate them to alter their behavior. Clearly, the impact of planning varies from one setting to another. Generally, it is easier to accept strategies that do not involve the termination of personnel than those that require dismissals. However, even on campuses where it is politically difficult in the absence of a fiscal crisis to earmark activities for retrenchment, it is possible to establish guidelines for retrenchment or reallocation in anticipation of fiscal hard times.

There is strong evidence that it is difficult to perform more than short-term planning during a fiscal crisis. Donald K. Smith comments on the experience of the University of Wisconsin System during the 1970s:

> It is all but impossible to do effective midrange or long-range planning for a state system of higher education in the presence of continuing fiscal crises and the kinds of coping actions and improvisations such crises generate . . . the disproportions between those actions which might be most wise in the long run, and those actions which may be necessary in order to cope with the crises, become increasingly clear.[2]

Thus, planning to minimize the negative effects of financial stress must be a mid- to long-range activity. In the short term, institutions usually can achieve only modest economies by reducing nonpersonnel expenditures for items such as travel, telephone usage, utilities, equipment, and supplies. Some short-term economies, such as reducing library purchases of books and periodicals, deferring maintenance and renovations, and deferring the purchase of replacement equipment, may in the long term cause severe financial problems or seriously undermine programs and facilities. Rain that falls through roofs that are not repaired, for example, can damage sensitive equipment. This is why large reductions can usually be realized only by reducing personnel costs. The larger the budget reduction or reallocation sought, the more time will be required to reduce personnel costs through attrition rather than by dismissal.

In responding to fiscal crises, faculty and administrators must be sensitive to legal constraints and external factors. Collective bargaining agreements, for example, limit the options available. State governments have become more involved in personnel matters in public higher education, introducing another level of actors into the planning process. For example, state-level involvement may extend from the negotiation of faculty contracts to control over the number of faculty and staff positions.

Under some budget formulas, institutional income may be affected by adjustments in instructional methodologies or staffing patterns, such as shifts from laboratory-intensive to lecture-intensive instruction or changes in the distribution of faculty ranks. Finally, special attention needs to be given to the resources associated with programs of diversity and affirmative action.

There is an obvious correlation between institutional size and the ability to reallocate resources and absorb losses. Larger institutions tend to have more "organizational slack," or flexible resources, than smaller ones. Those slack resources can be buried in programs and support services spanning the full range of priorities. That is why an across-the-board reduction as the initial retrenchment or reallocation strategy in larger institutions can often be absorbed without serious damage to programs.

The responses of specific institutions to financial hard times have been as diverse as the universe of American higher education. James Mingle catalogues a pattern of institutional responses to cutbacks based on an institution's perception of the severity of fiscal conditions;[3] Sigmund G. Ginsburg has a list of 120 suggestions for increasing institutional income and decreasing institutional expenses.[4] Some cutback or reallocation strategies are adopted more for their relative ease of implementation than for their appropriateness in addressing a particular situation. The precise strategies for implementation will vary from institution to institution and must be debated and evaluated according to institutional values and general principles and standards of legal and ethical behavior. No one strategy can be undertaken by itself or necessarily to the exclusion of others. When there is a fiscal crisis, a number of activities and budget lines might be eliminated completely in the short term before personnel retrenchment is begun. For example, one may wish to reduce the travel budget substantially before making any personnel reductions, but in the long run one would not wish to eliminate a travel budget completely before reducing personnel because of the importance of communication and interaction among faculty members and their peers.

In considering retrenchment strategies, institutions are cautioned that reducing support staff too severely may undermine the integrity of programs and services. Support staff lack the tenure enjoyed by most faculty, and are thereby more easily separated from the institution in times of scarce resources. However, a core of support staff must remain if the faculty are to accomplish their instructional, research, and public service missions. Although the expanded use of personal computers has reduced the need for some clerical assistance, and voice mail reduces the need for persons to answer every telephone, faculty cannot do everything by themselves. To maintain a core of support services, it may be appropriate to manage part of any reduction or reallocation by using the resources associated with vacant faculty positions. It may also be appropriate to consolidate support services geographically. Instead of having one staff for each department, a building might have one staff for all occupants. Typically, faculty are involved in decisions concerning the allocation of resources, especially at the departmental level; they cannot place an unfair burden of reductions on individuals who do not participate in the decision making.

Institutional strategies typically can be grouped into short-term (one to three years) and long-term (more than three years). These strategies can be pursued simultaneously in accordance with general principles suggested by Robert M. O'Neil that have been expanded upon based on more recent experiences with resource adjustments.[5]

Planning should involve everyone. Experience has shown that durable decisions require active faculty participation. However, because staff and students are often most directly affected by retrenchment and reallocation, they should participate in the process that makes recommendations about the distribution of programs and support services.

Participants should have access to all available information. Planners should be sensitive to the implications of information, especially when it pertains to personnel and programs. Understandings should be reached concerning the confidentiality of information. It is particularly important to identify the size of the financial problem it and, when appropriate, to translate that into faculty and staff positions and support allocations. Nothing focuses attention during deliberations about program priorities like detailed projections of budget reductions as they affect people.

Planning should not ignore the principles and traditions of the institution; short-term departures from such principles should be avoided. The long-term implications of major changes should be carefully considered, especially if the changes will affect the institution's character. This does not argue against strategies to reshape an institution, but rather calls for recognition of institutional strengths in certain traditions.

The institution's governing board and, in a system of institutions, central administrative staff, should be kept well informed of the progress of fiscal planning. Educating the regents or trustees and central administration is a wise investment of time that will be repaid with support for proposed policies and procedures. Similarly, significant friends of the institution, including alumni, donors, and local supporters, should be kept abreast of changes in programmatic direction.

The impact of the media should be taken into account. Journalists are very concerned about the plight of terminated staff and faculty, and are especially receptive to the issue of intellectual freedom. A process that involves faculty, staff, and students, includes broad consultation, and provides regular opportunities for public briefings will be seen as less controversial by the media.

In public higher education the state legislature should not be ignored. Legislators who are informed about actions that institutions take to remain financially and programmatically stable will tend to be more sensitive to institutional interests as state-level policy is being set. Institutional policy makers have to resist the natural inclination to shield the planning process from outside actors.

Faculty and administrative planners should project the long-term effect of retrenchment strategies before implementing them to ensure that the changes are desirable. A simple but effective approach is to trace the impact of decisions through several different scenarios.

Short-Term Strategies

In the short term (see figure 5.1), institutions can save money simply by reducing their day-to-day expenditures or can strive to increase income by earning a better return on their investments. On the expense side, institutions can usually achieve modest savings by curtailing expenditures for supplies, communication, travel, and equipment, unless they have experienced fiscal stringency for several consecutive years. Maintenance can be deferred, but with potentially severe long-term consequences. On the income side, the investment of institutional balances in short-term notes or interest-bearing accounts can be managed more closely to increase returns.

Larger short-terms savings can be achieved by carefully managing the number of faculty and staff. Faculty positions that become vacant can be held vacant, filled with lower-salaried faculty, or filled with temporary or part-time faculty. Fewer classes and larger sections can be scheduled. The number of sections offered of certain courses can be reduced. Staff positions can be held vacant.

Short-term budget reduction strategies tend to be administered across the board. Stanford University used an across-the-board productivity cut of 1 percent annually. Units could request special allocations from the reallocation pool if the allocations were justified by improvements in productivity. Other institutions use annual assessments to reallocate resources on a current-year basis. The advantage of an assessment as opposed to a permanent reduction in budget is that a unit has the flexibility to achieve the target in a different manner each year to fit changing circumstances.

Imposing the same burden on all units on short notice is more palatable politically than making selective reductions. However, across-the-board reductions strike strong and weak programs alike; the long-term effect may be to undermine the institution's strong programs. In addition, not all programs and activities start with the same degree of organizational slack. An across-the-board reduction of uniform percentage does not recognize differences among program budget bases. Institutions that have enjoyed rich support historically can usually withstand the negative effects of across-the-board reductions if the reductions do not continue for many budget cycles.

Figure 5.1   Short-Term Strategies for Retrenchment

□   Reduce day-to-day expenditures
□   Defer maintenance
□   Increase financial returns
□   Manage the number of faculty and staff
□   Enact across-the-board budget cuts

The administration of selective reductions requires strong leadership from both faculty and administrators. It also requires a framework of program priorities and a clear understanding of the resources required to maintain and improve programs. The political costs of exercising this kind of leadership must be weighed against the institutional costs of absorbing across-the-board reductions. If the institution has a sufficiently rich base, or if the reductions are not severe or long lasting, an across-the-board approach does have the advantage of maintaining peace if short-term economies must be achieved. Also, it may be appropriate to impose across-the-board reductions for the current fiscal year only to allow sufficient time to plan for long-term selective reductions.

The advantage of short-term strategies is that savings can be realized quickly. There are several disadvantages, however. First, the savings that can be achieved without significant pain tend to be a relatively small fraction of the total institutional budget. Larger reductions are more painful. Second, some long-term damage may be done to programs or facilities. If large numbers of vacant positions are filled by temporary or part-time faculty, for example, the composition and character of the faculty can be altered markedly. Programs that require senior faculty leadership, but have none because of vacancies, may wither. Faculty contact with students may be reduced. Using temporary or part-time faculty only adds to the breed of "gypsy scholars." Commitment to institutional research and service to both the institution and the community suffer. Furthermore, position vacancies do not always occur in programs slated for shrinkage in the long term. To meet student and programmatic demands, it may be necessary to replace some departing faculty with permanent appointments, thereby diminishing potential savings.

Long-Term Strategies

All institutions should have an academic plan in place. The academic plan sets the context for establishing program priorities for instruction, research, and public service, and by extension the priorities for support programs. Some institutions employ a strategic plan in tandem with the academic plan. The academic plan is a statement of what the institution will and will not do, and identifies the criteria for selection; the strategic plan presents the steps to achieve the academic plan, including guidance for the distribution of resources. Without the guiding principles of an academic plan, an institution will be hard pressed to change its allocation of resources in an intelligent manner.

Institutions faced with the prospect of reducing budgets significantly, or with the need to reallocate resources internally, must review their academic programs and nonacademic support activities carefully (see figure 5.2). To achieve economies and maintain or strengthen the quality of the institution, program review must be an active process with a regular schedule of reviews. Support activities should also be subject to periodic review. A common schedule for reviews is every five years. Review criteria for academic and support programs should address the following aspects of each program.

- ☐ Centrality to the institution's mission
- ☐ Service load
- ☐ Program uniqueness
- ☐ Enrollment demand (for academic programs)
- ☐ Quality and productivity
- ☐ Program costs

The academic plan provides the framework for reviewing the distribution of resources, while information garnered from program reviews describes how well the program array is satisfying that plan.

Significant reductions or reallocations of resources call for aggressive reviews of plans and programs. Generally, passive program shrinkage or elimination through faculty and staff attrition is not sufficient to meet

---

Figure 5.2   Long-Term Strategies for Retrenchment

- ☐ Review programs continually and aggressively, based on the academic and strategic plans
- ☐ Change staffing patterns through the following mechanisms:
  - —Early retirement incentives
  - —Part-time tenure
  - —External placement
  - —Retraining programs
  - —Leave policies
- ☐ Practice effective resource allocation

---

resource targets. Normal attrition may be the least disruptive way to cope with program shrinkage politically, but it is not selective. Faculty and staff do not leave only low-priority, mediocre-quality, or low-demand programs and support activities. In addition, with job mobility on the wane because of a static national economy, normal attrition usually will not free resources quickly enough to satisfy the demands of retrenchment and reallocation.

Large budgetary adjustments require changes in staffing patterns. Thus, retrenchment and reallocation strategies must focus on personnel policies and procedures. One avenue is to alter the policies and procedures providing faculty and staff with financial incentives to retire early, resign, or take unpaid leaves of absence. As with most retrenchment strategies, the objective is to provide institutions with budget-reduction alternatives to forced terminations. Ideally, the least productive and least needed faculty and staff would be the ones to depart under such programs. In reality, however, some of the best individuals will depart, too, because they are highly marketable and in demand. Moreover, unless used in conjunction with program review, these strategies do not earmark the programs and support activities that are lowest in priority and from which it is most desirable to encourage departures. Departments can be decimated by the departure of the core of the intellectual leadership. Of course, vacancies created when productive individuals depart can be filled with less expensive though qualified candidates. But this takes time, and programs can suffer in the meanwhile. Under the best of conditions the strategies listed below would be introduced without the threat of dismissal hanging over the heads of individuals.

Personnel actions are a delicate subject. Ideally faculty and staff should not be pressured to accept modified terms of employment. A healthy respect for due process on the part of officials will minimize the possibility of coercion and ensure that the individuals who are offered alternate employment programs have a primary role in selecting the programs. It is also important for faculty and staff to realize that not every suggested change in personnel status should be viewed as an adversarial situation. Many changes in personnel programs are entered into by mutual agreement. Implementation of the following strategies is discussed in detail by Mordechai Kreinin[6] and Carl Patton.[7]

Early retirement incentives. Faculty and staff who meet certain age or service criteria can be offered a lump-sum separation allowance for agreeing to retire or resign early. For example, Stanford University recently offered professors a single payment of double their base annual salary upon retirement. Benefits such as pension contributions, medical and dental insurance, and tuition allowances could be negotiated as part of the package. Another early retirement option is a liberalization of early retirement actuarial differences, whereby the institution buys up part of or all of the differences in pension benefits. The University of California, for example, included three early retirement programs in consecutive fiscal years that offered, in the most attractive version, five years of service credit and three years of age credit toward retirement. Institutions can also offer supplemental pensions to be paid from savings accruing to the vacant position. A further inducement to retire is the promise to hire retiring faculty and staff on a part-time basis for an agreed-upon period. Rehiring after retirement is governed by Internal Revenue Service guidelines.

There are several potential problems with early retirement systems. First, it may be necessary to convince governing board members in public and independent institutions and legislators in public systems that early retirement programs are valid uses of institutional or state funds and will save money. Some states may have legislation that prohibits the use of public money for such purposes. The rules of some retirement systems may have to be altered to enable individuals to take advantage of early retirement. Second, early retirement incentives may tempt some excellent faculty and staff to depart. To surmount this difficulty, one can design the incentive structure to discourage the best individuals from leaving. For example, severance salaries may be set at the average salary for a particular age cohort on the assumption that the best individuals in the cohort earn more than the average salary. It may be necessary to offer early retirement incentives only to faculty and staff in programs and support activities that have been earmarked for shrinkage.

Early retirement programs have significant front-end costs such as the package of severance pay plus benefits. However, the direct cost may still be less than that for outright dismissals, which often require one to two years' notice before they become effective.

Early retirement programs have had mixed success. A program developed at Michigan State University largely prevented forced terminations

during the 1981–82 academic year.[8] The University of California lost
thousands of senior faculty and staff as a consequence of three early retirement packages offered from 1991 to 1994. Leadership and institutional memory were lost in some academic programs and support
functions. Institutions with a relatively youthful faculty and staff profile
have few individuals interested in early retirement. Moreover, the impact of early retirement programs on the retirement rate is likely to be
substantial when they are first introduced. Generally, after an initial
swell, the overall retirement rate declines.

Part-time tenure (partial buyout). Under this idea, faculty and staff are
permitted to choose part-time appointments for any number of years up
to a predetermined maximum (e.g., five years). They receive a proportionate salary but have some of their benefits package covered in full. To
make this option more attractive, the institution can count each year under the arrangement as a full-time employment year for purposes of retirement and sabbatical leave.

Senior faculty and staff find this program more appealing than do
junior personnel. Senior individuals are more likely to be able to afford a
reduced salary because other options are open to them. Accordingly,
new junior faculty and staff can enter the ranks. Because senior faculty
and staff typically have higher salaries than their junior colleagues, the
savings from this strategy will be greater if senior personnel make up a
majority of those who take advantage of it.

External placement. To encourage less productive faculty and staff to
leave, an institution can pay for the cost of placement in positions outside the institution. This strategy benefits both the institution and the individual. Costs may include the services of testing and counseling
agencies and fees charged by position-finders. The costs of relocation
could be paid from savings that accrue to the vacant faculty or staff position. (Such costs probably will be much less than severance payments.)
Carl Patton suggests that to protect academic due process, the option of
external placement should be offered to all individuals within programs
earmarked for reduction.[9]

The manner in which faculty and staff are identified and approached for this arrangement requires considerable sensitivity, with the
assurance of academic due process and acknowledgement of the faculty's

primary role in determining questions of faculty status. Because this strategy focuses attention on individuals, not many will likely take advantage of it.

Midcareer change. A small number of institutions have implemented programs for midcareer change. These programs are designed either to retain faculty for other positions within the institution, or to provide support during the transition from academic to nonacademic employment. Retraining programs designed to keep faculty within the institution are aimed at individuals in academic programs that are shrinking, being eliminated, or changing focus. Selected faculty are given their regular salary plus funds to cover the costs of relocation, tuition, and other expenses associated with a graduate program. A retraining program usually permits one semester or one year of study. Although some individuals do receive advanced degrees, the programs generally are not designed to accomplish this. Those participating in the program have typically negotiated for placement elsewhere in the institution prior to their retraining. Some programs reorient faculty within a discipline (e.g., providing them with computer skills) to accommodate shifts in emphasis, the introduction of new technologies, and changing student demand.

Other programs are geared to retraining faculty and staff for employment elsewhere. Institutions may provide individuals with full or partial salaries for a limited period while retraining is taking place. A variation is the guaranteed income option for individuals moving directly to outside positions. With this option, the institution can guarantee for a limited period the difference between the individual's current salary and the salary of the new job. The concept can be modified to fit individual cases. For example, the institution can guarantee the full salary difference the first year and some fraction of the difference in later years.

As with the other strategies, trustees and legislators may have to be convinced that the program is an appropriate use of institutional resources.

Leaves. Modest savings can be achieved by altering leave policies. Institutions can encourage or require faculty members to take full-year sabbatical leaves at half-pay by withdrawing the option of one semester at full pay available at many institutions. Long Island University offered two-thirds salary for one year as an incentive for year-long sabbaticals and limited the number of one-semester sabbaticals to one-half the total number of all sabbatical leaves. Institutions can negotiate leaves of absence that provide a certain percentage of a faculty member's salary. Some of the money saved may have to be used to hire temporary replacement instructors; the balance represents the net savings to the institution.

Other strategies. Over a period of several years all 12- or 11-month faculty appointments can be reduced to 10- or 9-month appointments; or all faculty and staff can be furloughed for several days or annual faculty and staff salaries can be reduced by a small percentage. Because these arrangements would be mandatory, they would have to be administered across the board.

In general, these and other budget-reduction strategies that require alterations in institutional personnel policies and procedures will be most attractive to faculty and staff if the risks associated with career transitions are minimized. Planners must project each strategy's break-even point (i.e., where the cost of the program equals the salaries saved) to ensure that savings are achieved.

Any unilateral actions by administrators may place generally accepted principles of tenure and academic due process at risk. Financial savings should not be the only consideration when implementing new personnel policies and procedures; the need to maintain professional relationships is equally important.

Financial Exigency, Financial Stringency, and Retrenchment Policy

In some financial crises, college and university officials consider the prospect of releasing permanent faculty and staff as a way to achieve financial equilibrium, whereby the institution is able to operate without deficits. Regardless of the origin of the crisis or the numbers and kinds of individuals identified for layoff or termination, the separation of individuals from institutions is a painful process and one to be avoided if at all possible. Ideally, officials can solve an institution's fiscal problems through avenues other than releasing permanent faculty and staff. Sometimes, however, the magnitude of the reductions that must be accomplished within a very short period makes the release of permanent personnel unavoidable.

The termination of faculty is particularly difficult in that most institutions maintain a strong commitment to tenure and attempt to adhere to American Association of University Professors' (AAUP) principles and guidelines on academic freedom and tenure. The AAUP guidelines, which oppose the dismissal of faculty or the termination of appointments before the end of specified terms, except when stated conditions (i.e., "financial exigency") exist, are designed to prevent administrators from using financial exigency as a justification for capricious actions. Although these guidelines provide a general definition of financial exigency, it is necessary to interpret them and adapt them to specific institutional settings.

The Commission on Academic Affairs of the American Council on Education has expressed several concerns with AAUP's "Recommended Institutional Regulations."[10] The commission notes that the regulations state that terminations for financial exigency are legitimate only when the whole institution is on the verge of bankruptcy, and that terminations for program discontinuance are legitimate only when the program has been discontinued "based essentially upon educational considerations" that do not include "cyclical or temporary variations in enrollment" or financial stringency. The commission also argues that the definition of financial exigency and the conditions under which programs may be discontinued are too general to be practicable. Moreover, the commission is concerned that the vagueness of the definition of financial exigency encourages the courts to provide their own definitions that might differ from the definitions to which the institutions subscribe in good faith.

In the coming years it seems likely that some institutions will face the "edge-of-the-cliff" travails of bankruptcy, but that the great majority will face two less severe situations: a debilitating though not immediately life-threatening reduction of revenues such as state appropriations or tuition; and the need to reallocate resources internally. The focus of the debate about resource allocation, especially in hard times, is whether reallocation can in some instances be done on educational grounds to strengthen good programs and on the basis of enrollments and finances.

Although the central question concerns guidelines for reallocation, the debate is often about labels. At Michigan State University in 1980, for example, administrators chose the term "financial crisis" rather than "financial exigency" to describe the financial situation, arguing that because the institution was public, it was not in danger of collapse but rather of having its academic quality eroded by adverse financial conditions. The substantive issues are the degree of financial emergency and the procedures to be followed in reallocating and reducing resources.

Ralph Brown notes that cyclical enrollment variations are not grounds for program discontinuance. He argues against "a pernicious practice, extensively employed in large state systems, of measuring appropriations by formulas that reflect minute fluctuations in enrollments. The intent is doubtless to measure competing claims objectively, but the result must be harmful to stability of employment or of program."[11] Purely enrollment-driven funding formulas are not desirable, particularly in times of declining enrollments. However, they are the mechanism some states use to set appropriations for higher education. Most states consider enrollments in some fashion in establishing levels of state support. Legislators can and do cut the budgets of public institutions for a variety of reasons; institutions try to incorporate such possibilities into their fiscal planning.

Donald Cell argues in favor of accepting enrollments and the academic values that originate from disciplinary frameworks as legitimate components of what the AAUP terms "educational policy." With respect to enrollments, Cell states that "consideration of enrollment should...not be routinely dismissed by such negative code words as 'market' or 'financial'; enrollments more fundamentally reflect values held by students which, while we sometimes need to challenge them in the classroom, we should at the same time respect."[12]

Clearly, the quality of academic programs is a significant determinant in resource decisions. A program of mediocre quality and with low enrollments, for example, might drain resources from better programs. It might be necessary to boost sagging institutional enrollments by reallocating resources to make particular programs more attractive to potential students.

Difficulties arising from the internal reallocation of resources probably will touch more campuses than any other fiscal problem. The bitterness surrounding the proposed reallocation of resources at the University of Missouri during the 1981–82 academic year illustrates the magnitude of the potential problem.[13]

The major issue in reallocation is what to do with personnel in all categories: tenured, nontenured, and staff. AAUP guidelines address the elimination of entire academic programs but do not permit, short of financial exigency, the discontinuance of particular tenured faculty because of reduction in scope or reorganization of academic units. In a small institution that holds instruction as its primary mission, for example, enrollments might be insufficient to justify a five-person, fully tenured art history department. If the institution wishes to reduce its commitment to art history and wishes also to follow AAUP guidelines, its only alternative is to disband the entire program. Moreover, the institution would have to justify the discontinuance of the art history program "essentially upon educational considerations," by which is meant other than enrollment considerations. In dealing with low-demand or low-quality programs, there may be alternatives to the termination of tenured faculty members. If sufficient lead time exists, the size of the program faculty and staff can be allowed to diminish through natural attrition. In some situations faculty members can be redeployed or retrained. During any retrenchment of academic programs, the institution must maintain a commitment to students already enrolled in the programs.

The elusiveness of agreement about the definition of financial exigency is an indication that social, economic, and political forces are pressuring institutions of higher education to such an extent that many of the boundaries between normal operations and the AAUP definition of financial exigency are blurred. To deal with this problem, governance strategies are being advanced. Cell makes the following suggestions for providing the maximum protection of tenure while recognizing the financial realities many institutions face:

☐ The burden should fall on administrators to show that less harmful economies have been exhausted before the termination of permanent faculty and staff is called for;

☐ It is the responsibility of an appropriate faculty committee to determine which academic programs should be cut; and

☐ Within a program, tenured positions should have preferred status over untenured positions except when a serious distortion of the curriculum would result.[14]

The Long View

Program planning is a long-term, continuous activity because of the complexity of the academic enterprise and the need to involve administrators and appropriate faculty bodies. An orderly planning process typically includes at least five elements before programs reviews are initiated.

- ☐ Development of campuswide or systemwide policies and procedures and statements of priorities
- ☐ Development of institutional mission statements
- ☐ Establishment of personnel rules
- ☐ Establishment of planning principles
- ☐ Establishment of criteria and policies and procedures for the review of new and existing programs and activities

Although fiscal conditions ultimately are the force behind reallocation and retrenchment processes on most campuses, finances are often overshadowed by well-placed concern for personnel policies and procedures, especially faculty and staff welfare and legal rights and program review criteria.

Program reduction has obvious fiscal and political costs and is a drain on morale. These costs must be compared with cost savings and other benefits such as the ability to respond to enrollment pressures and to hire quality faculty. Institutions sensitive to the professional development of faculty and staff associated with programs and support activities about to be reduced or terminated will bear some of the cost of retraining, early retirement programs, and external placement. If faculty and staff must be terminated, the institution must take on the costs of severance agreements. Some faculty and staff will contest their dismissals in court; institutions must be prepared to assume the costs associated with these lawsuits. In general, the amount of personnel-related costs will depend on arrangements made for the personnel. When the University of Michigan closed its Department of Population Planning some years ago, for example, it honored its contractual obligations and reassigned tenured faculty to other programs. Accordingly, the savings gained from termination of the program and the costs associated with termination were not as great as if tenured faculty had been released.

Program reduction or elimination may be a consequence of enrollment decline; the institution must anticipate the loss of revenues from tuition and fees and, in the case of public institutions, the loss of some state appropriations. Public institutions may not be allowed to reinvest the savings that accrue through retrenchment in other programs and activities. Finally, programs that are heavily supported by external funds may require considerable institutional funds if they are to be continued, yet may yield few immediate savings if they are reduced or terminated. The potential future cost of continuing such programs must be carefully considered.

Other costs of reallocation and retrenchment may be more subtle. Faculty may not wish to be associated with a smaller program and may seek employment elsewhere, further eroding the core of program faculty. For example, if an institution reduces the scope of a program from the Ph.D. to the master's level, as has happened in several state public systems, faculty whose primary interest is in doctoral training and research may not be satisfied with teaching at the undergraduate and master's levels. Specific programs may have outside benefactors or supporters who may not want to be associated with a losing cause and may sever their ties with the institution if their programs are affected. Thus, one criterion for program evaluation must be external support and visibility. Similarly, certain programs may have special political connections. A political figure may serve on an advisory board of the program, or the program may serve a special state or regional political interest such as economic development.

In terms of diminished political support, the institution as a whole bears the cost of reducing or eliminating such a program. Within the institution, retrenchment and reallocation may cause disruptions in faculty governance unless faculty are closely involved in establishing policies and procedures well in advance of a financial crisis. Even if review criteria and policies and procedures for faculty and staff are set, governance groups become reluctant to earmark specific programs or individuals when the time arises. Morale problems arise in institutions undergoing faculty and staff retrenchment. Faculty who have provided long and useful service to the institution suddenly find themselves unwanted. If, for example, faculty terminations are decided on the basis of seniority, schisms can develop between junior and senior faculty. Reallocation and retrenchment may also push faculty or staff toward collective bargaining as a way to clarify relevant policies and procedures. Adverse media publicity about program reductions may exacerbate enrollment declines. Finally, situations involving reallocation and retrenchment may uncover deficiencies in administrative leadership, the knowledge of which ultimately may prove advantageous to the health of the institution.

The economics of reallocation and retrenchment require that long-term plans be made for programs and activities, which in turn must be held accountable for meeting plan objectives. In the academic arena, enrollments may have to be restricted so that the desired level of service can be provided with available resources. Enrollments can be controlled by rationing plans that have special admissions criteria for potential students in high-demand programs. Long-range enrollment targets can be established for all academic programs so that planners can better gauge future resource needs. Programs can be held to the targets, and those that fail to meet them can be subject to a loss of resources.

Long-term enrollment targets can be accompanied by projected staffing patterns. Institutions can project the impact of enrollment levels on decisions about promotion, nonretention, tenure profile, and external hiring of junior and senior staff, with the objective of making future staffing decisions more orderly.

Plans for program reduction and resource reallocation should also anticipate changes in programs and activities. If, for example, an academic program is to be phased out, arrangements must be made to accommodate students in the program. If tenured faculty in the program being eliminated are to be placed elsewhere in the institution, places must be made for them. The elimination of one degree program will affect other programs that depend on the eliminated one for courses offered or student enrollments. The impact of reallocation and retrenchment on diversity and affirmative action plans must also be projected in the areas of student enrollments and staffing.

Some institutions develop long-term reallocation plans in anticipation of financial hard times and enrollment shifts or declines: the University of Michigan established a Priority Fund for reallocation purposes. All units in the university had their base budgets reduced 1 percent each year to provide a pool of resources for the fund. All programs and activities had an opportunity to compete for money in the fund, although allocations were made only to those with the highest priority.

Clearly, if institutions are to adapt, most will have to reallocate resources at some time. Whether the reallocations are done in response to fiscal crises or through the desire to maintain or improve the quality of the institution, they will have to be made selectively. When institutions first encounter financial stringency, they can manage the situations most painlessly through across-the-board reductions. After several years of financial hard times, however, the strongest programs and activities can no longer be penalized at the same rate as the weakest ones. Selectivity in accordance with an institution's academic mission and goals should be the guiding factor in retrenchment and reallocation, whether the institution establishes detailed targets centrally or assigns broad targets to large units such as colleges and schools that are then permitted to determine the detailed targets. Above all, the process of reallocation must be sensitive to the character and academic mission of the institution and must involve members of the campus community.

For Further Reading

The literature on retrenchment and reallocation continues to grow as the national condition of diminishing resources for higher education becomes the rule rather than the exception. William F. Lasher and Deborah L. Greene review the literature on retrenchment and reallocation in "College and University Budgeting: What Do We Know? What Do We Need to Know?" in John C. Smart, ed., *Higher Education: Handbook of Theory and Research*, Vol. IX (Edison, NJ: Agathon Press, 1993). Two NACUBO publications that include case studies for retrenchment and reallocation are *Practical Approaches to Rightsizing* (Washington, DC: National Association of College and University Business Officers, 1992) and James A. Hyatt, Carol Herrnstadt Shulman, and Aurora A. Santiago, *Reallocation: Strategies for Effective Resource Management* (Washington, DC: National Association of College and University Business Officers, 1984).

J. Fredericks Volkwein examines the relationship between state regulatory policies for public higher education and financial flexibility in "State Regulation and Campus Autonomy," in John C. Smart, ed., *Higher Education: Handbook of Theory and Research*, Vol. IV (Edison, NJ: Agathon Press, 1988).

Raymond F. Zammuto discusses "Managing Decline in American Higher Education," in John C. Smart, ed., *Higher Education: Handbook of Theory and Research*, Vol. II (Edison, NJ: Agathon Press, 1986). Similarly, Kenneth P. Mortimer and Barbara E. Taylor examine "Budget

Strategies Under Conditions of Decline," in Larry L. Leslie, ed., *Responding to New Realities in Funding,* New Directions for Institutional Research no. 43 (San Francisco: Jossey-Bass, Inc., 1984). The uses of comparative data are discussed in Carol Frances, ed., *Successful Responses to Financial Difficulty,* New Directions for Higher Education no. 38 (San Francisco: Jossey-Bass, Inc., 1982).

A number of early references are still valuable for the insights they provide. An excellent collection of papers appears in James R. Mingle et al., *Challenges of Retrenchment: Strategies for Consolidating Programs, Cutting Costs, and Reallocating Resources* (San Francisco: Jossey-Bass, Inc., 1981). A summary of the major issues addressed by Mingle and his colleagues is found in "Redirecting Higher Education in a Time of Budget Reduction," *Issues in Higher Education, no. 18* (Atlanta: Southern Regional Education Board, 1982).

A thoughtful paper on retrenchment in a large institution is Donald K. Smith's "Coping, Improving, and Planning for the Future During Fiscal Decline: A Case Study from the University of Wisconsin Experience," in Martin Kaplan, ed., *The Monday Morning Experience: Report from the Boyer Workshop on State University Systems* (New York: Aspen Institute for Humanistic Studies, 1976).

In the 1970s the American Association for Higher Education (AAHE) published two monographs on retrenchment: Marjorie C. Mix's *Tenure and Termination in Financial Exigency,* AAHE/ERIC Higher Education Research Report no. 3 (Washington, DC: American Association for Higher Education, 1978) discusses the legal aspects of financial exigency; and Kenneth P. Mortimer and Michael L. Tierney examine the administration of resource reallocation and retrenchment in *The Three "R's" of the Eighties: Reduction, Reallocation, and Retrenchment,* AAHE/ERIC Higher Education Report no. 4 (Washington, DC: American Association for Higher Education, 1979).

The position of the American Association of University Professors (AAUP) on tenure, academic freedom, and financial exigency is stated in several classic documents: William Van Alstyne, "Tenure: A Summary, Explanation, and 'Defense,'" *AAUP Bulletin 57, no. 2* (June 1971): 328–333; Ralph S. Brown, Jr., "Financial Exigency," *AAUP Bulletin 62, no. 1* (April 1976): 5–16; and Kingman Brewster Jr. "On Tenure," *AAUP Bulletin 58, no. 4* (December 1972): 381–383. The AAUP publication *Academe* regularly reports on these matters.

Notes

1. Paul Strohm, "Faculty Responsibilities and Rights During Retrenchment," in James R. Mingle, et al., *Challenges of Retrenchment: Strategies for Consolidating Programs, Cutting Costs, and Reallocating Resources* (San Francisco: Jossey-Bass, Inc., 1977), pp. 134–152.
2. Donald K. Smith, "Coping, Improving, and Planning for the Future During Fiscal Decline: A Case Study from the University of Wisconsin Experience," in Martin Kaplan, ed., *The Monday Morning Experience: Report from the Boyer Workshop on State University Systems* (New York: Aspen Institute for Humanistic Studies, 1976), pp. 25–40.
3. James R. Mingle, "Redirecting Higher Education in a Time of Budget Reduction," in *Issues in Higher Education no. 18*, (Atlanta: Southern Regional Education Board, 1982).
4. Sigmund G. Ginsburg, "120 Ways to Increase Income and Decrease Expenses," in *Business Officer 16 no. 6* (December 1982): 14–16.
5. Robert M. O'Neil, "A President Perspective," in *Academe 69, no. 1* (January–February 1983): 17–20.
6. Mordechai E. Kreinin, "Point of View: For a University in Financial Trouble, a Faculty 'Buy-Out' Plan Can Save Money and Face," in *The Chronicle of Higher Education*, January 27, 1982, p. 56; and Mordechai E. Kreinin, "Preserving Tenure Commitments in Hard Times: The Michigan State Experience," in *Academe 68, no. 2* (March–April 1982): 37–45.
7. Carl V. Patton, *Academe in Transition: Mid-Career Change or Early Retirement* (Cambridge, MA: Abt Books, 1979); and "Voluntary Alternatives to Forced Termination," in *Academe 69, no. 1* (January–February 1983): 1a–8a.
8. For the details of the Michigan State University experience, see Kreinin, "Point of View" and "Preserving Tenure Commitments in Hard Time," and Collette Moser, Roy Matthews, and Marvin Grandstaff, "Buyouts at MSU," in *Academe 68, no. 5* (September–October 1982): 6.
9. Patton, "Voluntary Alternatives to Forced Termination."
10. W. Todd Furniss, "The 1976 AAUP Retrenchment Policy," in *Educational Record 55, no. 3* (Summer 1974): 159–170.
11. Ralph S. Brown, Jr., "Financial Exigency," in *AAUP Bulletin 62, no. 1* (April 1976): 3.
12. Donald C. Cell, "Opening Question-Raising Remarks: Tenure and Exigency Problems," paper presented at AAUP Conference on Hard Times, Washington, DC, May 20, 1982.
13. Paul Desruisseaux, "Missouri Campus Bitterly Divided over How to 'Reallocate' Funds," in *The Chronicle of Higher Education*, May 19, 1982, p. 1, 12.
14. Cell.

APPENDIX
Approaches to Budgeting

This appendix briefly describes several approaches to budgeting: incremental budgeting; planning, programming, and budgeting systems; zero-base budgeting; performance budgeting; formula budgeting; and cost-center budgeting. These approaches are not mutually exclusive; aspects of each may overlap. However, each approach is distinctive in its focus and in its emphasis on different kinds of information.

Incremental budgeting focuses primarily on increases or decreases rather than on the budget base, which presumably has been examined in total or in part in previous years. Planning, programming, and budgeting systems weigh the costs and benefits of programs and activities and thereby focus on their substance. Zero-base budgeting examines all programs and activities each budget cycle. Performance budgeting focuses on measures of program or activity performance. Formula budgeting is concerned mainly with the "fair share" distribution of resources among institutions as determined by quantitative measures. Finally, cost-center budgeting calls attention to the relative ability of a unit to be self-supporting.

Incremental Budgeting

It is difficult to avoid the playful definition that incremental budgeting is how most individuals, departments, and institutions manage their resources most of the time. That is, the financial situations of most individuals, departments, and institutions usually change only modestly from one budget cycle to another. This observation allows for the possibility that individual or organizational fortunes may advance or decline. Because the change in financial resources from one fiscal year to another is generally small compared with the financial resource base of the previous year, the way in which individuals and organizations spend their resources typically varies only at the margin from one budget cycle to another. The pattern of expenditures for most individuals, departments, and institutions is largely determined by continuing commitments.

The largest component of any institutional budget is salaries and benefits, often accounting for up to 80 percent of the total annual operating budget. Unlike manufacturing and some service industries, higher education does not have significant fluctuations in its workforce over short periods of time. (For political and economic reasons it is often extremely difficult to upset these commitments.) Changes in the base budget from one budget cycle to another tend to be too small to have a major impact on historical spending patterns.

This is not to argue that significant fluctuations in the amounts of resources available or in the demands placed on available resources do not occur from one fiscal year to another. For example, an oil crisis that drives up the cost of energy or a large loss of tuition income resulting from an unanticipated enrollment decline could lead to major reductions in expenditures. Such changes would not be considered incremental or decremental.

Incrementalism is as much a framework for analyzing organizational or political behavior as it is an empirical description. Political scientist Charles E. Lindblom characterizes incrementalism as "the science of muddling through."[1] In any organization or political arena the key actors usually have different priorities and different value systems that sometimes conflict. An organization's direction is arrived at through a complex array of often uncoordinated negotiations among the key actors. Frequently the only way to accommodate competing plans is to make changes at the margin only. Also, when the costs of gathering information are high or when there is considerable uncertainty about the future, organizations tend to move cautiously through modest changes (i.e., to avoid any negative unanticipated consequences of major changes, organizations make adjustments at the margin). Most organizations, like most individuals, seek a stable existence.

In the literature of political science in general and budgeting in particular there has been considerable criticism of the incremental approach to decision making. Some observers, including Lance T. LeLoup, have examined the literature of empirical studies in budgeting and argue that though major changes in policy direction are made by organizations, those changes are at times masked by historical budget data.[2] Other criticisms come from the normative perspective: incrementalism does not encourage rational examination of the full spectrum of policy choices and selection of the best one; the objective of incremental decision making is to minimize conflict rather than to make the best policy choice; incremental budgeting does not examine the budget base or the array of existing fiscal commitments, but focuses on changes to those commitments; and incrementalism is driven more by political demands than by analytical assessments of requirements.

The weaknesses of incremental budgeting are also its strengths. It is simpler, more natural, easier to apply, more controllable, more adaptable, and more flexible than modern alternatives such as program-planning budgeting, zero-base budgeting, and indexed entitlements. The fact that traditional incremental budgeting has endured while several budget innovations have had minimal success speaks to the strengths of the incremental approach.

Planning, Programming, and Budgeting Systems

Planning, programming, and budgeting systems (PPBS) evolved in the early 1960s from a number of concepts and techniques that emerged from the methodology of quantitative analysis: operations research, economic analysis, general systems theory, and systems analysis. The PPBS approach systematically links the planning process to the allocation of resources. Several characteristics of PPBS are its macroeconomic perspective, its focus on centralized decision making, its long-range orientation, and its systematic analysis of alternative choices in terms of relative costs and benefits.

The primary conceptual components of the PPBS approach are the program budget and cost-benefit analysis. A program budget organizes and presents information about the costs and benefits of an organization's activities (i.e., programs). A program plan establishes goals and objectives for the organization and relates them to the organization's activities. The costs and benefits of alternative ways of reaching the goals and objectives are established through an examination of resource requirements and estimated benefits to be gained from alternative programs. An important aspect of the program budget is projection of the costs and outputs of programs over a number of years to provide a long-term view of the fiscal implications of those programs.

The cost-benefit aspect of PPBS involves a rigorous quantitative analysis of policy alternatives. Goals and objectives and their desired degree of achievement must be quantified, as must the costs and benefits of policy alternatives.

The PPBS concept has generally been more appealing on paper than in practice. The federal government experimented with PPBS in the Defense Department in the early 1960s and expanded the concept to other federal agencies. However, the federal bureaucracy did not assimilate the PPBS framework and the system died. Several state governments and institutions have also experimented with PPBS or modifications without noteworthy success. However, the positive features of the PPBS approach continue to encourage other governments and organizations to experiment with it. Those features include grouping activities by function to obtain output-oriented cost information; estimating future expenditures in cases where multiyear commitments are made; and quantitatively evaluating situations where it is necessary to screen policy alternatives.

The disadvantages of PPBS are numerous. The approach calls for strong central management in that it requires agreement to be reached on goals and objectives. In some settings, particularly in higher education institutions, it is difficult to reach an understanding of what constitutes a program. It is also difficult to establish specific outcomes for programs that may have joint outcomes. PPBS focuses more on what must be accomplished than on operational tools for implementing goals and objectives. Program accounting often yields information of limited value because it reflects arbitrary cost allocations that are frequently not supported by the accounting systems. A particularly troublesome limitation is that, while it makes sense conceptually to aggregate activities in programs, most organizations are not structured by program: a program usually cuts across several organizational units. In most cases resources are allocated by organizational unit rather than by program because there is greater accountability in units. With the responsibility for programs spread across several organizational units, it is difficult to control the flow of resources on the basis of program needs. Generally, it is easier to distribute resources to organizational units on the basis of functional needs (e.g., instruction, research, service, physical plant maintenance, and academic support) and to control resources on the same basis.

PPBS also assumes considerable knowledge of the organization and its future direction. The costs associated with collecting this information and performing detailed analyses of alternative plans can be significant.

Zero-Base Budgeting

Zero-base budgeting is a rationalist decision-making procedure with a microeconomic focus. In contrast to the centralized PPBS approach, zero-base budgeting is initiated at the lowest levels in an organization. It assumes no budgets from prior years; instead, each year's budget is started from a base of zero. Each budget unit in the organization evaluates its goals and objectives and justifies its activities in terms of both the benefits of the activities and the consequences of not performing the activities. This evaluation is in the form of a decision package, which includes a description of the activity, a definition of alternative levels of activity (including minimum and maximum levels), measures of performance, and costs and benefits. Decision packages at one level of the organization are ranked in priority order and forwarded to the next level of review. Each package in turn is ranked at successively higher administrative levels and decisions are made regarding the distribution of resources to each unit.

The most obvious disadvantage of zero-base budgeting, and the one most often cited when the method has been put into practice, is that it assumes no budget history. Thus, it does not recognize that some commitments are truly continuing ones (e.g., to tenured faculty and key staff) and cannot be readily altered in a short period. Most labor-intensive organizations, especially colleges and universities, cannot initiate and terminate activities quickly. Accordingly, when organizations attempt zero-base budgeting, they assume a fixed base of support (e.g., 80 percent of the previous year's budget) and apply the zero-base techniques to the balance of the budget. This strategy compromises one of the purported advantages of the method, namely, the elimination of a protected budget base.

Practitioners of zero-base budgeting claim that they gain a much better understanding of their organization through the preparation and review of the decision packages than they would using other budgeting methods. However, zero-base budgeting requires a great amount of time and paperwork, and it is sometimes difficult for all the actors involved to reach agreement on priorities. Another complaint is that the centralized preaudit of lower-level decisions robs those levels of decision-making autonomy and responsibility. Some observers argue that periodic program reviews are a more practical way to carry out the positive aspects of zero-base budgeting.

Performance Budgeting

During the early development of public administration budget and planning, the budget was viewed as an instrument of expenditure control. Performance budgeting, which emerged in the late 1940s, represented a shift to a management orientation by focusing on programs and activities that became ends in themselves. Performance budgeting addresses activities rather than objectives, and performance budgets consist of activity classifications, performance measurements, and performance evaluations. Clearly, the intent of performance budgeting is to improve efficiency.

In recent years there has been a rebirth of interest in this technique, particularly at the state level. In the newer form of performance budgeting, resources (inputs) are related to activities (structure) and results (outcomes). Specific outcome measures are defined in both qualitative and quantitative terms. Accounting structures relate expenditures of resources to results. Explicit indicators of input/output relationships or indexes relating resources to outcomes are defined. Goals are specified in terms of performance measures (i.e., desired input/output ratios).

Difficulties have arisen in applying the newer forms of performance budgeting in the public arena: the development of performance measures has often flowed from the state level down to the institutional level; outcome indicators are sometimes viewed as useless or controversial because they are linked with program budgets at high levels of aggregation;

quantitative measures are more widely employed than qualitative measures; and performance measures at high levels of program aggregation are not easily linked with centers of administrative responsibility. Performance budgeting also often lacks political appeal from the point of view of legislators. Opponents of this method argue that the rational orientation of performance budgeting reduces the amount of influence participants can bring to bear. Legislators also dislike the complexity and volume of budget documentation.

Tennessee, which experimented with performance budgeting as part of its more traditional formula budgeting approach, has the oldest program of its kind. A small fraction of the state budget for higher education was appropriated to the Tennessee Higher Education Commission for allocation to individual institutions based on proposals for improved instructional performance. What began as a pilot program in the 1970s grew to encompass 5 percent of the total operating budget by 1983 and 5.5 percent, or $17.5 million, by fiscal year 1990.[3]

Formula Budgeting

Formula budgeting is a procedure for estimating resource requirements through the relationships between program demand and program cost. These relationships are frequently expressed as mathematical formulations that can be as simple as a single student-faculty ratio or as complicated as an array of costs per student credit hour by discipline for many levels of instruction (e.g., lower division, upper division, master's, doctoral). The bases of budget formulas can be historical data, projected trends, or parameters negotiated to provide desired levels of funding. Budget formulas are a combination of technical judgments and political agreements.

Budget formulas come in all shapes and sizes. Most are based in some way on enrollment or student credit hour productivity data. Within the same overall framework, different formulas usually address the distinct functional areas of an institution's operations. Thus, instructional resources may be requested on the basis of average faculty teaching loads or credit hour costs by student level or course level, applied against historical or projected enrollment levels. Library support may be requested on the basis of enrollments and service relationships. Requests for support of maintenance and physical plant may not be enrollment-based at all, because the operation of the physical plant is a fixed expense relatively immune to shifts in enrollment. Accordingly, the physical plant formulas are probably based on square footage of facilities and the nature of the facilities.

Some budget formula frameworks do not use distinct formulas for different functional areas. The base method of formula budgeting computes the resource needs for a base function, usually instruction, based on enrollments and instructional costs or workloads, and then computes the needs of the other functional areas (e.g., libraries, academic support, maintenance and physical plant) as a percentage of the base. On the other hand, the staffing pattern method of formula budgeting computes only salary expenditures for the institution. Nonsalary budget requirements can be determined by other methods (e.g., incremental budgeting).

In general, budget formulas are used on a systemwide or statewide basis for state-supported institutions as a foundation for generating budget requests. Formulas tend not to be used as a means to distribute resources within an institution, however. By their very nature, budget formulas are simplified models of how institutions operate. This modeling role of budget formulas sometimes puzzles state officials who assume that funds appropriated to institutions should be spent in exactly the same manner as requested through the formulas.

It is not uncommon for a formula-generated budget request to exceed the amount of available state resources. In such cases the formula may be modified to yield a request consistent with available resources, or state officials may simply allocate a percentage of the formula-generated amount.

A number of factors usually are considered by those evaluating alternative formulas. How many portions of institutional budget requests are generated by budget formulas? How closely does the state adhere to the formula-generated request? Do the budget formulas recognize different types of institutions? What is the inherent incentive structure of the budget formulas? (For example, in the instructional area does doctoral-level instruction receive a significantly higher weighting than undergraduate instruction? Does the formula for maintenance and physical plant provide an advantage to a certain type of facility?) Are formula parameters derived from historical data, norms, or projections? How does the formula treat different levels of instruction? Does the formula differentiate among disciplines?

The advantages and disadvantages of formula budgeting have been debated for three decades. Budget formulas were introduced during higher education's growth in the 1950s and 1960s as a means to ensure the equitable and rational distribution of resources. The quantitative nature of most budget formulas gives them the appearance, if not always the reality, of objectivity. Budget formulas tend to reduce conflict in the budget process in that they represent agreed-upon rules for the distribution of available resources. This conflict reduction occurs in part because budget formulas have become a mechanism for relieving legislators of the pressures of institutional lobbying campaigns. By pointing to the formulas, legislators can disclaim control of institutional allocations. At the same time, budget formulas have enhanced institutional autonomy by lowering the level of political influence in budgeting. Budget formulas have also reduced the uncertainty inherent in the budget process by helping institutions and state officials predict needs for future budget cycles. The budget process is simplified in that the same decision rules (i.e., budget formulas) are used from one budget cycle to another.

As with any quantified approach to decision making, there are disadvantages to formula budgeting. Formulas based on historical data, for example, discourage new programs or rearrangements of existing programs. Any new program is at a disadvantage until it has accumulated its own history. Formulas that are applied across a number of institutions are criticized for encouraging homogeneity and mediocrity (critics assume that funding is provided on the basis of some average). Formulas tend to be based on average factors (e.g., costs or enrollments) rather than on marginal ones and thereby favor institutions with increasing enrollments. That is, as enrollments increase, institutions gain more resources than they "deserve" because of the average-factor base. For the same reason, as enrollments decline, institutions lose resources faster than they should. Consequently, some states are seeking formulas that distinguish between fixed and variable costs.

Formulas become restrictive if state officials assume that appropriated resources are to be used in institutions in the same patterns as in the formula-generated budget requests. Formulas are also restrictive in the sense that once they are put in place, many are difficult to modify significantly because user expectations have solidified.

Responsibility-Center Budgeting

Responsibility-center budgeting, also known as cost-center budgeting or more informally as "every tub on its own bottom" budgeting, is intended to focus primary responsibility for the management of resources on schools and colleges within the university. In doing so, the emphasis is shifted from budgetary control to program performance.

In this model schools and colleges become revenue and cost centers. Revenues are attributed to each school or college, including tuition and fees, research funds, indirect costs from research, gifts, and endowment income. In addition to the direct costs of the academic unit, such as salaries and operating expenses, the units are responsible for a share of the indirect costs of the university, including the operation and maintenance of the physical plant, utilities, the library, and general administration.

Responsibility-center budgeting also requires the taxing of schools and colleges to create a central "subvention" pool to support academic units without sufficient revenues of their own. Thus, the central administration continues to be involved in key resource decisions. It is not unusual for a college of letters and science with a large instructional service workload in support of other schools and colleges, to have insufficient revenue of its own to be self-supporting. Accordingly, part of the tax charged the other schools and colleges goes to fund the service mission of that college.

Responsibility-center budgeting forces institutions to ask questions about how revenues should be credited and the degree to which central services should be funded. All support services are fully costed; all academic units are credited with their share of total institutional revenue. Some of the advantages include the incentive to enhance revenues and manage costs; an appreciation of the total costs of the enterprise; a recognition of the importance of tuition revenue; and the development of explicit charges for space-related costs causes a reappraisal of the need for, and value of, space. In addition, the explicit portrayal of indirect costs helps reinforce the idea that indirect cost recoveries are to cover real costs and the portrayal of income and expenses at the college and departmental levels substantively involves the faculty and staff.

Responsibility for managing resources implies that surpluses will be carried forward from one fiscal year to the next, and that deficits are liabilities against future years' budgets. Responsibility-center budgeting encourages the removal of central controls and gives attention to performance or outcome measures. The budgeting system also makes it clear that academic decisions have financial consequences. It offers the incentive that more ownership in the enterprise will encourage entrepreneurship. Schools and colleges expect central administrative services to be more responsive; if academic units are to be held accountable for generating revenues and managing costs, administrative units should be held accountable for delivering services at a reasonable price.

Responsibility-center budgeting carries with it the danger that attention will be focused exclusively on the bottom line, whereby academic performance and priorities are sacrificed for fiscal considerations only. The potential exists for suboptimization, in that schools and colleges may seek to maximize revenues to the detriment of the entire campus. Increased revenues usually bring with them increased indirect costs. Schools and colleges may tend to expand local services that duplicate central services. To avoid this possibility, central services need to be managed carefully.

The campus community in public institutions has a very different perspective on how institutions acquire resources than in independent institutions. This perception has made it more difficult to implement responsibility-center budgeting in the public sector.

For Further Reading

William F. Lasher and Deborah L. Greene provide good summaries of the different types of budget strategies in "College and University Budgeting: What Do We Know? What Do We Need to Know?" in John C. Smart, ed., *Higher Education: Handbook of Theory and Research*, Vol. IX (Edison, NJ: Agathon Press, 1993). Aaron Wildavsky reviews some of the budgetary innovations such as program budgeting and zero-base budgeting in *The New Politics of the Budgetary Process*, 2nd ed. (New York: HarperCollins, 1992).

Richard J. Meisinger Jr. examines formula budgeting in *State Budgeting for Higher Education: The Uses of Formulas* (Berkeley, CA: Center for Research and Development in Higher Education, University of California, 1976). The technical aspects of the formulas discussed in the monograph are dated, but the conceptual framework for budget formulas is still applicable. See also Paul T. Brinkman, "Formula Budgeting: The Fourth Decade," in Larry L. Leslie, ed., *Responding to New Realities in Funding*, New Directions for Institutional Research, no. 43 (San Francisco: Jossey-Bass, Inc., 1984).

Richard H. Allen reviews incentive funding in "New Approaches to Incentive Funding," in Larry L. Leslie, ed., *Responding to New Realities in Funding*, New Directions for Institutional Research, no. 43 (San Francisco: Jossey-Bass, Inc., 1984). See also Anthony W. Morgan, "The Politics and Policies of Selective Funding: The Case of State-Level Quality Incentives," *The Review of Higher Education 15, no. 3* (Spring 1992): 289–306, for a discussion of state-level incentives in four states.

Edward L. Whalen thoroughly examines responsibility-center budgeting in *Responsibility-Center Budgeting* (Bloomington, IN: Indiana University Press, 1991).

Notes

1. Charles E. Lindblom, "The Science of 'Muddling Through,'" *Public Administration Review XIX* (Spring 1959): 79–88.
2. Lance T. LeLoup, "The Myth of Incrementalism: Analytical Choices in Budgetary Theory," in *Polity 10*, no. 6 (Summer 1978): 488–509.
3. Anthony W. Morgan, "The Politics and Policies of Selective Funding: The Case of State-Level Quality Incentives," *The Review of Higher Education 15*, no. 3 (Spring 1993): 292.

Index